Praise for *The De*

"The church exists in order to tell a story about dying.
This book feels as though it is written out of real strength and deep
anchorage, to show us how to tell that story so as to invite people to
see how they belong in it and it belongs in them, in all their chaotic
humanity. Poignant narratives are woven into a surefooted theological vision with grace and conviction. A book to generate the right
kind of confidence in the gospel—humble, realistic, celebratory."
— Rowan Williams, 104th archbishop of
Canterbury, theologian, and poet

"You know how we love to tell the story. Well, this book is story that
loves to be told. It is a story about a Presbyterian congregation
that found new life by giving itself away. It is a story of Marty and his
slow advance to death by cancer, in the bosom of the church. It is a
story of little Owen, who understood his baptism: 'Death can't get
me, because Jesus has got me.' The curator of this story is Kara Root,
who herself has come to understand the work of a pastor in the best
ways. It turns out that this story is about the God who shows up in
surprise with transformative gifts. The reader will cherish this well-
written book and come to discern that the 'old old story' is always yet
again becoming our 'new new song.'"
— Walter Brueggemann, Columbia Theological Seminary

"Kara Root has an exquisite gift for paying attention to and then
speaking of what she sees, showing us along the way that there is
sacrament in the telling of our stories. *The Deepest Belonging* illuminates the ache and the grace that come as we enter into those stories
with one another. Most of all, it beautifully bears witness to the love
that—stubbornly, wondrously—holds us through everything."
— Jan Richardson, author of *Sparrow: A Book of Life and Death and Life*

"In a time of increasing anxiety and divisiveness, *The Deepest Belonging*
offers true comfort and hope. From the flesh and blood of pastoring
real people, Root tenderly, poetically, and authentically responds to
the quiet yearnings of the human soul. This is simply the best book
of Christian faith I've read in over a decade."
— Mark Yaconelli, executive director of
The Hearth, author of *The Gift of Hard Things*

"Kara Root is the pastor everyone wants and needs. Quicksilver smart, deeply honest, and blessed with a gift for language, she invites us all into a deeper exploration of our faith. *The Deepest Belonging*, part memoir and part pastoral journal, shines a bright light on the vital questions of faith: What is God up to here? How can we pay attention? How do we join in with God's activity in the world? To read this book is to be given a gift."

—Thomas G. Long, Candler School of Theology, Emory University

"When I am asked for an example of a pastor in a small, traditional church that has managed creative and sustainable change, I tell stories of Kara Root. Her pastoral work shines with integrity and love. I couldn't be more thrilled that she is now offering her wisdom to us all in *The Deepest Belonging*. This is a real treasure."

—Nadia Bolz-Weber, author, Lutheran minister, public theologian

"This book is a gift of the most precious kind. To those of us who have given our lives to the local church, here is the most healing reminder that what we do matters. Whatever their shape, however small or ordinary they be, communities of faith and belonging matter. However robust or fragile our calling to their leadership, our witness to God's truth and presence in all of life matters. In reading this book, my own vocation has been renewed, and I am grateful."

—Simon Carey Holt, pastor of Collins Street
Baptist Church, Melbourne, Australia; author of
God Next Door: Spirituality and Mission in the Neighbourhood
and *Heaven All around Us: Discovering God in Everyday Life*

"It is a gift to read the stories of Kara Root and her church, both of whom live and lead with courage and honesty."

—Jodi Houge, pastor and church planter,
Humble Walk Lutheran Church, St. Paul, MN

"Christians of our generation have been tasked with reviving a dying model of church. With heartbreaking honesty, Kara Root parallels her personal and pastoral narratives with the narrative of church. Rather than emerging hopeless, Root's work illuminates how the liturgical practices of our faith are not just rituals; they are the means by which we know that Death with a capital *D* does not have the last word on life."

—Mandy Sloan McDow, senior minister,
Los Angeles First United Methodist Church

The Deepest Belonging

The Deepest Belonging

A Story about Discovering
Where God Meets Us

———

KARA K. ROOT

Fortress Press
Minneapolis

THE DEEPEST BELONGING
A Story about Discovering Where God Meets Us

Scripture quotations, unless otherwise indicated, are from the New Revised Standard Version Bible © 1989 Division of Christian Education of the National Council of the Churches of Christ in the United States of America. Used by permission.

Scripture quotations marked MSG are taken from *THE MESSAGE*, copyright © 1993, 2002, 2018 by Eugene H. Peterson. Used by permission of NavPress. All rights reserved. Represented by Tyndale House Publishers, a Division of Tyndale House Ministries.

"Lazarus Blessing" © Jan Richardson from *Circle of Grace: A Book of Blessings for the Seasons* (Orlando, FL: Wanton Gospeller Press). Used by permission. janrichardson.com

Spirit, Open My Heart. Words: Ruth C. Duck; copyright © 1996 The Pilgrim Press, Cleveland, Ohio. All rights reserved. Used by permission.

"Who Am I?," in *Letters and Papers from Prison*, Dietrich Bonhoeffer Works, vol. 8, ed. John deGruchy, trans. I. Best, L. Dahill, R. Krauss, and N. Lukens (Minneapolis: Fortress Press, 2009), 459. Used by permission.

Every effort has been made to trace the copyright holders and obtain permission to reproduce this material. Please do get in touch with any inquiries or information relating to rights.

Cover Image: "Everyone" by Holly Welch
Cover Design: Brad Norr Design

Print ISBN: 978-1-5064-7093-1
Ebook ISBN: 978-1-5064-7095-5

Owen and Maisy, this is for you.

Listen to your life. See it for the
fathomless mystery that it is.

In the boredom and pain of it no less than
in the excitement and gladness:

touch, taste, smell your way to the
holy and hidden heart of it

because in the last analysis all
moments are key moments,

and life itself is grace.

—FREDERICK BUECHNER,
Now and Then

Contents

Preface

My friend Lisa Larges recently called me "a homiletical creature." She explained, "You have an agenda (and I certainly don't mean this in a negative way), not teaching or explaining, but witnessing to a truth. It undergirds your understanding of both leadership and ministry." Since she said that, I've been turning the phrase over in my mind and picturing myself as a "homiletical creature." What kind of creature is a homiletical creature? I imagine an impish, whimsical being with big eyes and big ears wide open, taking in the world, absorbing and processing encounters and moments for the messages they hold, and then going around sharing them with its big mouth. That's the friend perspective. The kid perspective might be that Mom is always preaching, even when she's not in the pulpit. Our poor kids can't make it through a dinner without their professor dad and pastor mom theologically musing about something. But the idea of being a homiletical creature has grown on me. I've decided to own it.

The world is brimming with beauty and significance. I want to pay attention. Life is a sermon I want to be listening to. What is God saying to me through my experiences? How does a particular situation point me toward God? What responses do these sermons from the Divine call out in me?

So Lisa is right—I do have an agenda. I want to see and hear God in all things, to watch for the places God meets us, to tell about and join in the work God is doing. And this agenda does undergird my leadership and ministry. This book is an exploration of how watching for God and seeking to join in God's work came to be my agenda, to shape my leadership, and to form how the congregation I serve understands ministry.

This book tells stories of discovering how God meets us. It presumes that God does meet us. It presumes that we can be met by God. Reflecting on my life and telling stories from my congregation begins, for me, in the belief that every life, every congregation has stories of being met by God. So I hope the book invites you to watch for and tell those stories yourself. I think a world full of homiletical creatures would be a delightful place to live indeed.

Thank you to my editor, Beth Gaede, for her patience and encouragement and for thinking it was "fun" to go back and forth many times to find the exact best wording for something. Thank you to my manuscript readers for your feedback and suggestions that made this book so much stronger: Jason Carle, whose extraordinary intuitive pastoring inspires and teaches me; Lisa Larges, whose humor, insight, and camaraderie help me pastor as I wish to more often than not; Theresa

Latini, a fellow homiletical creature, who is always up for picking apart situations for the theological insights and then draws me even deeper; and Jamie Schultz, whose friendship and support are a mainstay of my daily life.

To Lake Nokomis Presbyterian Church, thank you for your faithfulness and honesty, for your vulnerability and your courage. It is my great honor and joy to minister alongside you. I have learned so much from our journey together. Thank you for entrusting me with your stories. You once told me you know how to be the church. Thank you for continuing to teach me what you know.

Most especially, thank you to my husband, Andy. After my serving as reader and proofreader for some nineteen of his books, he was so eager to see this book come to life and find its place in the world. I've given my love of grammar and wordsmithing to his projects, and he gave his dedicated discipline and freakish ability to structure time to my project. I could not have finished this book without his wholehearted support. For more than twenty years, we've helped each other ask good questions, dig deep, and stay grounded, watching for what God is doing and trying to understand the deeper messages in the world. I am profoundly grateful for you. Thank you for shaping a homiletical life together with me.

Introduction

O nce upon a time, there was a most remarkable storyteller. Singular, unequaled in creativity and prose, master of subtlety and
surprise. This storyteller was unparalleled at the craft, weaving such
intricate and complex symphonies of plot and drama, centering on
the lives of characters so full and profound that even the most skilled
tellers of tales in the land could only strive to emulate this storyteller.

So inspired were the stories that every other author who wrote,
every poet who spoke out in verse, every composer who wove a myth
in music, every artist who sought with any medium at all to in some
way bring a fresh story into the world, inevitably plagiarized, so deep,
original, and imaginative were the works of this one prolific storyteller.

But this storyteller was mysterious. In fact, the storyteller's identity was shrouded in vagueness, and few and far between were those
who had ever claimed to see a face up close or hear a voice with their
own ears. People knew people who knew people who had talked to
people who had caught a glimpse of this author leaving a grocery store
or who thought they had driven past the writer's house, though no

one was quite sure exactly *where it was*, or even generally *where it might be*, *if the truth be told. So for the most part, the only peek into who this magnificent, unsurpassable weaver of tales was as a* person *was what people could glean from the stories themselves.*

The stories were analyzed and studied, both for their power as narratives and also for any clues of the storyteller's identity, glimpses into the soul of this great crafter of lives and plots. The most notable thing about these stories, those who scrutinized them would point out, was the common threads throughout all of them. Every story included pain and tragedy, every story bled real, messy life, but also every story was saturated with redemption. Hope shone out in intricate and always surprising ways.

And every story brought about its salvation through the most unlikely of characters. The heroes were never the strong, brave, and handsome, the winsome and wonderful. They were always *the overlooked, underrated, flawed, and forgotten. They were the weak and the strange, the inadequate and illogical.*

In fact, it was a favorite tactic of this storyteller to tell stories within stories, to surprise the characters themselves by their role in the stories, not knowing what was unfolding in and around them until they looked back—or not ever knowing in their own lifetime until their children or grandchildren looked back—and discovered that the hero was right there next to them the whole time. That redemption had unfolded right under their noses—in their own hands, in fact—without their being aware they were playing such a pivotal role.

The protagonists often hadn't a clue that the story was their own, and then once they realized it was, they discovered almost immediately afterward that it wasn't at all their story—that it was much larger than they were and might have unfolded entirely without them, except that it hinged completely on their very selves, and nobody else, occupying that particular role. This was one of the storyteller's trademarks.

Over time, the more astute students of this writer's work began to discover that the stories, while in and of themselves each beyond measure, fit together like a puzzle, that one story shed light into another, opened it up—made it more complete, actually—and most extraordinary of all, that every story belonged beside the other stories because they were actually just tiny chapters in a single, much larger Story (with a capital S) that this writer was creating.

And one day, when the whole corpus of this writer's work would be complete, the Story would be epic—comedy, tragedy, adventure, and romance, fanciful and heart-wrenchingly beautiful—and nothing would remain unresolved. It was building to the most satisfying and complete conclusion, one never before conceived of.

Also, they began to discern, the Story was highly autobiographical. Hidden within every element of every story that made up every part of this larger Story were revelations of its creator: the fingerprints, the breath and body and warmth, the glances and expressions and intonations and nuances, the tones and shades of the storyteller were next to each character, behind each situation, underneath every word. The stories and the Story were utterly about the storyteller

But the final shock of all, the greatest revelation came to the truly attentive readers, the unsuspecting ones who sat down with the story and opened their souls to it, who met the story face to face, heart to heart, who let it tell itself to them and wept and laughed along with the antiheroes. Those were the readers who saw, as they met each character, what the characters themselves could not see or could see only after time—that they were in this greater Story. That their choices and words, their tragedies and triumphs, not only were their own stories but became the very substance from which the larger Story took form, without which the larger Story could not be.

These particular readers would celebrate the characters, and marvel at the genius of the author, and be moved beyond measure at the power of the Story itself. Then they would close the book and put it down, intending to stand and stretch and move on to other business, but instead, they would be suddenly glued to their seats, hearts skipping a beat, unable to move for the astonishing realization that washed over and engulfed them, the bewildering insight that actually, their very own lives were part of the Story.

And the Story was real.

Chapter 1

When We Come Together, God Meets Us

It was easy to love God in all that was beautiful. The lesson of deeper knowledge, though, instructed me to embrace God in all things.

—SAINT FRANCIS OF ASSISI,
The Writings of St. Francis of Assisi

Spirit, open my heart
to the joy and pain of living.
As you love may I love,
in receiving and in giving.
Spirit, open my heart.

—RUTH DUCK, "Spirit, Open My Heart,"
Glory to God: The Presbyterian Hymnal

1

December 2015

*I*t was a cold Tuesday morning in December when Marty, highly agitated and visibly distressed, rushed into the church office. "Do you have a minute, Kara?" he asked.

He unzipped his heavy winter coat, pulled off his mittens, jerked a chair up to the desk, and shakily lowered himself into it. Reaching into his shirt pocket, he pulled out a folded piece of paper. With trembling hands, he gave it to me. "Could you look at this?"

I opened it. It was medical test results. For some time, Marty had had a cough and some tightness in his chest. Suspecting asthma, or something to do with the harsh Minnesota winter air perhaps, he had finally had some tests done the week before. Over the weekend, he'd gone online and viewed his results. Unable to reach his doctor, Marty had an appointment scheduled for Thursday—two days away. In the meantime, he had been carrying around this deeply creased printout of his test results next to his constricted chest. No longer able to bear the dread alone, he had driven over to the church building with them, and now he was handing them to me to read. "What do you think that means?" he asked, pleading.

I looked down at the paper in front of me. It was packed with words. But right in the center, the phrase rose up and nearly shouted off the page: *tumors too numerous to count.* My heart dropped into my stomach.

"I don't know, Marty," I answered. "It doesn't sound good, does it?"

I am a pastor.

It's a weird thing to be. It means people thrust test results under my nose and ask me what I make of them. It means they invite me to come over and anoint their belly the night before they go into the hospital to have a baby, because the last time they went into a maternity suite, their baby died, and they're terrified this time around. It means I sit across from people and invite them to tell me stories about their dead parents so I can plan their funerals, and I sit across from parents and invite them to breathe when they tell me about finding drugs in their teenager's laundry basket.

Being a pastor means I walk around all week mulling over a passage of the Bible—some story about Jesus, or a Psalm of David, or an admonition from the long-dead apostle Paul—until my own life and the world around me start to crack open and shed light into this Scripture, and vice versa. And then I sit on Friday and Saturday nights at my dining room table and pray and write until something appears and rearranges and aligns—and it feels mysterious and miraculous every time—to become a sermon I will stand up in front of people and preach.

Being a pastor means I'm self-employed for tax purposes, but I have dozens of bosses, with dozens of versions of my job description in their own minds, and lots of appreciation and gratitude, and lots of disappointment and frustration, and they're all happening simultaneously at every moment.

Being a pastor means I work in a dying institution that can't financially sustain itself, and yet year after year, we are still here. It means I work for a dying organization—a denomination—where all the well-thought-out structures, programs, and plans that flourished in decades past are crumbling and disappearing, and there is a general unease bordering on panic about what is going to become of this thing called "church."

Being a pastor means that I work in a dying institution in a time when the customs and voice of the church are seen as increasingly archaic and unnecessary; there are plenty of therapists, death doulas, event planners, funeral directors, and groups of friends willing to do the duties once reserved for clergy. My teenaged kid came home from school the other day and announced that he got ordained online during study hall. (While his ordination was effective immediately, he will be required to wait, per state law, until he's eighteen to officiate a wedding.) According to a recent Gallup poll, judges, day-care providers, police officers, pharmacists, medical doctors, grade school teachers, military officers, and nurses are all seen as more trustworthy than pastors.[1] Esteem for organized religion is waning, and amid a smorgasbord of spiritual and religious options, the Christian church, with its flagrant rancor and division, is appearing less and less enticing, or necessary.

But I love the church.[2] So much—really, *all*—of who I am is because of the church. It's my root system and the nest where I was fed and from which I was launched into the world. It's what I grappled with, and pushed away, and came back to, different, and saw with different eyes. I can't not be in the church; I can't not serve the church. Church is who I am.

Even so, experiences of church are not always life-giving, or even benign. Injury, hurt, rejection, and pain are wrapped up together with the beauty and hope that is church. Each human soul's fear, hypocrisy, power mongering, and myopia are writ large here. Mix these with the search for meaning and longing for truth, and the results can be dangerous. There are lots of reasons people don't stay, or leave and don't return to church. But I stayed. I returned.

I lost almost everything to get here. Who I thought I was, who I thought God was, how I believed life worked, and what I believed church to be. My path to pastor has not been simple or clean or kind. I journeyed first through death, as, I've learned, all the paths that lead to real life do. Truth is here, even though churches only brush up against it from time to time, and that often by accident. And goodness is here that doesn't come from—in fact, is quite apart from—all our striving to be good. The times I most feel my deep love for the church are when it's transcendent, mysterious, and unknowable and when it's messy, haphazard, and human. And my favorite moments of all are when it's all of these at the same time.

Church is a broken and messed-up collection of beautiful souls longing for the world to reflect the truth of God's love. These people show up to be with each other, believing there is a reason to come, a reason to risk, a reason not to quit. Just think of it! Each person wakes up on a Sunday morning (if that's when their congregation meets) and gets dressed, eats breakfast, gets into their car and drives, or takes a bus, or walks to this place and not another. Each person makes two dozen small choices in that direction, any one of which could shift the outcome. Each one chooses not to stay in bed, not to put on sweatpants and chip away at their to-do lists, not to turn the car in the other direction and do the grocery shopping instead, but to come to a gathering of people there to worship God. They come, in spite of a hundred other options, a hundred other ways to measure their day or parcel out their minutes, many of which may even feel more satisfying or productive. Even if they come just out of habit, underneath, somewhere, they believe church is a worthwhile use of their precious, limited time. Something in them believes they could receive something, or give something, or feel something, or learn something.

This is not a small thing. This thing we do called church, this *churching*. This trusting that God is real, trying to practice trusting that this is so, reminding each other that it is, is no small thing. Talking *to* God, even when it feels illogical; listening to stories from a book written centuries ago and cultures away as though it has something important to do with us, *to* us; repeating strange, ancient rituals with bread and wine; and engaging in institutional formalities with words like *elders* and *ministry*: these churching things we do, as church, help us know who we are. By coming together in this way, people are saying, *This is what I choose to help define my life, to be known as, to shape me in some way*. Even as so much around us changes, church is timeless, and deep, and it matters.

We are on a journey in this life. Sure, we are on a metaphorical journey, the kind people write poems about. But also, plain and simple, we come into this life, live it, and leave it; we are born, and we die. Every human life has a beginning, an end, and the span in between, however long or short that span may be. On this journey we are defined by two intertwined facts: we belong to God, and we belong to each other. Life includes lots of other ingredients, of course, but this is the inescapable essence of living a human life: we belong to

God, and we belong to each other. We can act as though one or the other of them is not real. We can avoid or deny part of our belonging, behaving as though we are in this life alone and against others, or ignoring our belonging to God completely. But that doesn't make either belonging not true. It just means we are disconnected or distracted, not sensing and living into our true human identity and connection at the moment.

We all have moments when we sense our deepest belonging; they often come without words. In the midst of a spectacular thunderstorm, we might feel the power and mystery of a universe far greater than ourselves. When we are lost in profound grief, someone's presence with us momentarily anchors us and holds us fast. In an otherwise ordinary day, a tiny pause, a bright, subtle detail, a flash of humor or joy can suddenly make our breath catch and make us feel like we're seeing beyond the surface into something true. Whether or not we acknowledge that God is there, whether or not we say out loud that we recognize our connection to all others, in experiences of inexplicable depth, surprising beauty, or great love, we are momentarily tasting our true belonging.

Church is those who acknowledge God is here and use words to say out loud our true connection to all others. Church is those who are human together—that is, we practice on purpose our real identity and our primary belonging: we remember whose we are, and we recognize who we are. Alongside other people, we lift our own souls to God, whose presence we acknowledge explicitly. Being church is remembering that we belong to God and we belong to each other. Being church does not mean coming to a building once a week, but by coming regularly and remembering together, we deepen our awareness of our belonging and practice trusting that it's true every day of our journey from birth to death.

All the people who show up have their own reasons for coming. This is the reason I come, the reason I keep showing up: because I want to be awake to what's real. I am letting church define and shape my life, because church makes me more human. It makes me more grateful. It keeps me attentive to the mystery. It opens me up to receive and live into the deepest belonging. And I've come to see and trust that when we humans come together and open our hearts—even a tiny bit for a tiny moment—to trust that there is something more, something transcendent, and that it even has something to do with us, God meets us. Every time. We already belong to God and to each other, so when we show up together with each other, God meets us.

Right around the time Marty wandered in and settled among us, we started saying just that aloud each week in worship. It feels too wonderful to grasp and too easy to forget, so we repeat it every time, "Wherever we are on our journey of faith, when we come together, God meets us." In worship, we name this ungraspable thing, this divine and human dinner party of the soul. God is, of course, present at all times and everywhere. But especially here, especially now, when we answer God's invitation and show up, God meets us. When we come to the set table prepared for us, ready to receive from our Divine host, God welcomes us and joins us here. I trust this completely, and I love church for this reason most of all.

So I'm a pastor. I have close to zero faith in institutions and lots of cynicism and impatience with organizations in general. I am not in this gig for doctrinal or even theological convictions, though certainly I have those. But this—that God is here, in every life, in every moment, tragedy, breakthrough, euphoric celebration, and ordinary second of boring monotony—this is what captures me. That every life is sacred to God, that every person's melody is written into the limitless symphony, and that when we come together, we hear a bit of God's eternal song playing out right now with us, *every time*—that is what has captured me. So it's what I have given my life to; it's my work as well as my belief. But it's a strange job, hard to understand, difficult to explain in a culture of concrete objectives, rational calculations, and measurable, upwardly mobile ambitions. To stand with people together in the possibility of being met by transcendence, to hold open space for Divine encounter, there is no category for that on a W-2.

My son, Owen, had a best friend, I will call him Ben, all through his elementary school years. Ben's parents were both doctors, and unlike anyone I had known well before, they had no religious affiliation at all and hadn't had at any point in their lives. As far as I knew they could point to no faith they'd grown up with and left, no family spiritual roots, no church baggage they were carrying or religious chips on their shoulders. They were part of a growing population who seemingly never gave God a second thought or ventured to dip a toe into religion, saw no reason or need for such a thing. They lived with a strong ethical system of compassion and responsibility that guided them well.

This difference between us popped up every so often. Ben was sometimes curious that Owen believed in God. His parents were undoubtedly curious that Owen's parents, who seemed like smart, ethical, rational people, both had careers in religion. Once, I saw his mom pause on my front porch and do a double take at the plaque we have hanging there: "Bidden or unbidden, God is present." Probably they had never met people like us before either.

One New Year's Eve we were together at a neighborhood party. Ben's mom was telling me about spending time with a dear friend of hers whose mother was dying. It was painful for her friend to watch her mom deteriorate, and the experience was weighing heavily on her friend, she said. Then she looked right at me, and her tone grew frank. "I've been wanting to ask you about this. Her pastor has been there a lot. He sits with her in the hospital sometimes and has really been supporting my friend." Then she looked at me with her curiosity wide open and asked, "Is *that* what you do?"

We are each on a journey in this world, making our way through life from our first breath to our last, walking alongside one another, and accompanied by God, in whom we find our beginning, our being, and our deepest belonging. This is being human. Some of us get to spend our paid time and our vocational energy remembering this and reminding others that it is true. We get to say, "When we come together, God meets us." This is being a pastor. I'm a curator for the community of the deepest belonging.

Right in front of me on this Tuesday morning was Marty, with his alarming test results gripped in his shaking fist, caught at that terriblest of human intersections, the one between fear and the unknown. And I was his pastor. Here we go.

Chapter 2

When We Lose Guarantees

Vulnerable we are, like an infant. We need each other's care or we will suffer.

> —SAINT CATHERINE OF SIENA,
> *Little Talks with God*

Abide in us, Lord God, that we may abide in You, locked to You, spirit to Spirit, in the deep mystery of God and humanity.

> —MARGARET CROPPER,
> *Evelyn Underhill's Prayerbook*

*F*ive years earlier, Marty had, in his words, "shown up one Sunday and never left." A nondescript, middle-aged man with thinning hair, glasses, and a toothbrush mustache, he was my stereotypical image of a small-town, general-store owner, the guy who knows where the Allen wrenches are stored and how to operate the key cutter. He was pleasant and unassuming. He had a stutter that cropped up every now and then, and I always admired how he'd just power through it without apology or explanation—even volunteering to read Scripture every year in our Good Friday service.

Cheerful, friendly, outgoing, and easygoing, Marty quickly became beloved—especially by the older women in our congregation. When he joined the church, they took him under their collective wing. He was quickly in demand as a willing-to-learn square-dancing partner, and they competed for opportunities to introduce him to their favorite stop on the robust Minneapolis church lutefisk dinner circuit.

I knew Marty had come back to his Presbyterian roots after a sharp veer into a conservative Baptist church as a teen and some recent years in a Unitarian church with his ex-wife. He sometimes vaguely referenced an apparently decades-long wild canter through pagan, Buddhist, new age, Wiccan, and other spiritualities, but this was so hard for me to imagine that I mostly didn't let it in. He had often commented on how he had valued and learned so much from his spiritual wanderings but had now come home to where he began. To where he belonged. This made more sense to me. He seemed like a decent-and-in-order Presbyterian. I could sooner imagine my own mother in a sequined body glove front and center at a Lizzo concert than I could picture Marty as a practicing Wiccan. But quietly eating lutefisk in a church basement alongside Dee and Sylvia? Absolutely.

There was nothing flashy about Marty. He was simple and straightforward, not the one to take the final bow, but a willing and happy member of the ensemble. In my own mind, he quickly became part of the supporting cast. It was as though he'd always been there.

When Marty became a member, our congregation had just adapted our liturgy for welcoming new members to reflect the truth that Jesus Christ, who is God with us and for us, *is* with us—actually, tangibly, right here *with us*—when we are with and for each other. We had also added one more question to the regular Presbyterian vows about being a follower of Jesus Christ and contributing to the ministry of the community. When Marty stood before the congregation to become a member, he was the first among us to be asked, "Will you allow us to be, for you and with you, the body of Christ in love and service, joy and suffering, sharing life and faith together?"

To this he had responded, smiling and steady, "I will."

Since that day Marty had served as an elder and as the church treasurer and had in countless other ways cared for this little church in which he'd felt so cared for. If the water cooler tank at the end of the hall was full, chances are it was because Marty had seen the jug getting empty and had carried it downstairs to refill it with fresh, filtered water. If light bulbs were out or screws were loose somewhere, Marty could be found on a weekday afternoon beside our patron saint of building care, Gary, replacing or tightening them. If someone was sick, they might get a call from Marty, just checking in to see how they were doing. If they needed a ride somewhere, they could count on Marty to offer it; he could fit lots of cheerful older ladies in his van. He'd just shown up one day and become part of the community. This is one of the surprising gifts of church. That this happens feels at once miraculous and fascinating.

We all knew Marty couldn't wait for retirement. He talked about it frequently and had big plans for his life after he finished working. After a couple of years of stressful unemployment, he now worked as a test-grader; it was solid work and mildly interesting. But his sights were set on retirement; that's what really fired up his imagination. "How long, Marty?" people would ask. "Six more months!" Marty would answer.

When Marty turned sixty-five, we placed on the communion table the white chocolate cupcake someone had thoughtfully brought in to celebrate his birthday, and we lit the candle. We sang "Happy Birthday," and he grinned and blew out the candle. But we knew that for Marty, this was more than a birthday. This was the moment for him to shift the trajectory of his life from here on out.

After worship, people clapped him on the back and congratulated him on his retirement. "What fun it will be to watch what you'll do!" *To watch the plans flow from the dreams you've been storing up!* But that is not what happened.

Instead, a few weeks later, Marty finally went to the doctor for his nagging cough. This was the visit he'd been postponing until after his sixty-fifth birthday, until Medicare could kick in and cover the costs. Instead of walking out of his job and into his next chapter in triumph, he walked into my office with his test results and terror. Instead of his future stretching out before him in untold delight and impending adventure, it slammed into him with shadowed unknowns.

The report he showed me turned out to be as bad as it appeared. Marty was diagnosed with stage 4 lung cancer.

Perhaps the deepest and most difficult question most of us spend a lifetime with is, *Who am I?* And just when we think we have a grasp on it, we change, and we have to wrestle with it anew. Who am I, now that my partner has died? Who am I, now that I have this diagnosis? Who am I, with this new-found freedom? this person to love? this job that inspires me? Who am I, now that I am suddenly responsible for this tiny new being? Who am I, when I've done something so horribly beyond what I thought I was capable of? When I can't take back those words, when I can't repair that breach? *Who am I when who I thought I was has changed?*

Who am I? is a scary question. And it almost never comes alone. If belonging to God is what it means to be human, then the very real extension of *Who am I?* is, *Who is God?* Who is God who would allow this to happen? Who is God in the midst of this? Who is God, if not who I thought God was? Who is God now that who I am is changing?

In Mark 8:27–38, Jesus asks his disciples, "Who do you say that I am?" I'm struck by the speed and confidence with which Peter responds, as though he has been mulling over this question in those moments of deep thought before sleep creeps up to deliver you. Peter has given up a perfectly stable career as a steady fisherman to follow this guy around, perhaps because this very question has so intrigued and compelled him. Now he's finally invited to issue his conclusion—and seems positively thrilled at being asked. He answers enthusiastically, "You are the Messiah."

And oh, it must feel *great* to say it out loud! It summarizes everything Peter has longed for—and all that he hasn't put words to until now. *God is saving us! Before my eyes every day, I see the promise made real—in his words, in his healing. This is it! He is it! We are being delivered from all that is broken. The fulfillment is here, and I am ready to declare it!*

So, face beaming in confidence and trust, he delivers his pronouncement. Most likely he is expecting a hug or some kind of praise for his astute observations. Affirmation, at least. *Yes, Peter, you hit the nail on the head, you (*affectionate gaze*).*

Instead, Jesus says, "What you say is true, I am the Messiah. But it doesn't mean what you think it means. I must undergo great suffering, be rejected by the religious rulers, humiliated in front of everyone, and killed. And after three days, I will rise again."

And this rattles Peter terribly. "Jesus, what are you saying? I've seen what you are! You are here to save us all! Stop this crazy talk!" *(You're stepping way outside the definition of you that I'm comfortable with.)*

And Jesus *sharply rebukes* him. I can't imagine the shock and pain for Peter when Jesus turns to him and says, "Get behind me, Satan! You are seeing things not as God does, but as humans do." Then Jesus calls the crowd around him and tells everyone what *Messiah* really means.

Who am I? the Savior asks. *Not your hero after all. I'm not the fulfillment of all your wishes and dreams, who ends your distress and solves all problems and makes everything better. I am not the one who saves you from life's pain and difficulty. I am the one who joins you in life's pain and difficulty.*

Life doesn't often turn out the way we think it will. Sometimes it's entirely contrary to our intentions for our lives. Pining for motherhood, we might find ourselves unable to bear children. Or the children we do have come with much different needs, or more challenging personalities, than we'd anticipated. Or they grow up and for whatever reason don't, or can't, leave our home. Or they leave us and never look back. We might have planned to marry and instead remain single. Or we might have planned to stay married but end up single again. Money, opportunity, health, support—we might not have whatever it takes to do what we wanted to do with our lives. Jobs, friendships, circumstances either beyond our control or completely our own fault shape a life quite divergent from what we had decided our path would be. More often than not, what we'd planned is not how things actually end up. God doesn't give us guarantees of health, success, or safety (and Jesus didn't have them either, it turns out). In fact, almost the only guarantee for being human is that we will die. This is certain and inevitable. Nearly everything else is up for grabs.

When our son, Owen, was born, my husband, Andy, was working on his PhD in practical theology at Princeton Seminary. We'd wanted a child for a while and were ecstatic over the pregnancy. In the delivery room, after the midwife said, "One more push!" Owen emerged into the world. They held up this screaming, purple stranger that was my son and placed him briefly on my chest for me to marvel at. Then they took him away to clean him off and weigh him while they finished with me. Swaddled and capped, he was placed into Andy's arms.

Andy looked into his son's eyes. Owen sucked his tiny fist and gazed thoughtfully back. Then Andy spoke to Owen—the first time Owen was directly addressed as a newly emerged human—and the first thing my child heard was about being human and what this life would hold. "Hi, Owen, I'm your daddy. Welcome to life! Being alive means that one day you are going to die." Clearly, life with a theologian dad meant getting right to the heart of it from the get-go. My erudite husband explained to his newborn son that facing death was what it meant to be human. Then, turning toward the window and gently bouncing this tiny boy, he whispered to him an impromptu song that became "Daddy's Lullaby to Owen" for years to come:

> Owen, dear,
> do not fear,
> do not fear, your daddy's here.
> You might be sad,
> you may be scared,
> but you're not alone.

When Jesus emerges from the warmth and safety of his own mother's womb into this world, tiny and screaming, wrapped in swaddling clothes and resting in his own daddy's arms, the same is true for him. *One day, Jesus, you are going to die. This is what it means to be human.*

The Messiah doesn't get to swing into this life and rescue people out of it without touching down. Every grief and separation boring into our gut he shares with us. With every breakdown of trust, loss, and tragedy wrought between us, every person who goes to bed hungry, angry, or painfully alone, he is there, holding us, joining us in it. At his first breath, his life is already entirely lost for our sake.

Jesus looks at his beloved disciples and at the crowds of people gathered around unaware of what is coming for him, frozen in this moment of incongruence, while they still see him as invincible savior and he sees the cross ahead. Then he pauses and takes a deep breath. Filled with the ache of loving them in all their misguided expectations, looking into all of their hope-filled faces, he shatters their illusions.

This Messiah gig is not all it's cracked up to be. Yes, I'm the Messiah. That means I belong to the world, to each and every one of you, and in me the whole world has its belonging.

"You who want to save your life will lose it. And you who lose your life for my sake will find it." *Following me is the death of self-protection and self-promotion; it's the end of the pursuit for invincibility and self-sufficiency. Following me is agreeing to a raw and often painful life, lived wide-awake and open to hurt.*

It means losing all you thought was your life and strength and dignity and purpose. It means being deeply, truly human.

This is a real life you're signing up for, Jesus wants them to know.

Following me means opening your heart like I have, to all the world, and to every beloved, befuddled mystery of a person made in the image of God. It means feeling the suffering they feel, taking on each other's burdens, standing with and for one another when the going is hard, accepting being misunderstood, persisting in loving, forgiving and being forgiven, being vulnerable and sometimes scared.

We spend so much of our energy saving our lives. Building up our armor. Crafting others' perceptions of us. Hiding the darkness and the weakness and the shame within us, protecting ourselves from the darkness around us. Pursuing safety and doing whatever we can to make ourselves feel secure. Dreaming and planning for a future that mostly lies just beyond our reach.

But when we let go, when we finally let ourselves be seen, when we allow the truth of our humanity to come to light, alongside each other, with and for each other, denying the false selves we construct, taking up our cross and following Jesus into the suffering of our own lives and sharing the suffering of others, when we lose our "life" and the control we thought we had to shape and protect it, we find our real life.

This is church. This is what church is and does. Church is the people who lose their lives and find them, who ask together, again and again, *Who am I? Who are you, God?* and let the answers awaken us to deeper life.

I was raised with an invincible-savior kind of faith. Bathed in a tonic of genuine kindness and doctrinal confidence, I received an immersion indoctrination of the very best kind: God loved me and had a wonderful plan for my life. This was affirmed in every Sunday school class and Sunday-morning church service, every Sunday-evening prayer service, and every Wednesday-night Awana club meeting throughout my childhood. Every verse I memorized and glued as a tiny jewel onto the gold crown on my Sparks vest reminded me of this. Every Joyful Noises kids' choir song my mom taught me and the dozens of other children and that we performed for the congregation with hands perfectly folded in front of our belly buttons reiterated this. The message was reinforced with regularly administered doses of church camp and vacation Bible school and later on, through a regional champion Bible quiz team, an active youth group that made annual mission trips, and a good, deep dunk in a Baptist Christian college education.

Strong and mighty, and ever attentive, God listened to prayers and intervened to save us in every dilemma, from Parkinson's to parking spots, if we only asked (in the right way and with the right intentions: *Your will be done, Lord*). I'd heard too many stories of miracles and Divine guidance from those around me and had too many personal experiences of God's loving presence to ever question such foundational truths.

My parents were "in the biz." For most of my childhood, my dad was a pastor at a small Christian Missionary Alliance church turned Evangelical megachurch. My dad and the other pastors were all dynamic, engaging, caring, and invincible men. In my childhood, our church of three hundred ballooned to eight thousand worshippers on any given weekend. In addition, my parents had a nonprofit ministry, which meant that my three younger sisters and I tagged along with them around the country to churches and camps. My mom did mime and "creative dramatics" with kids; my dad spoke to the adults from the books he'd written about grace, shame, chemical dependency, and dysfunctional family and church systems. He was a Midwest, Evangelical, minor church celebrity. And I was on the inside of it all. Church was where everybody knew my name—if not my first name, then for sure my last name—because of who my dad was.

I took pride in being the pastor's kid, speaker's kid, author's kid, church babysitter, youth volunteer, nursery worker, volunteer receptionist, nanny, resident assistant, project coordinator, teacher's aide, camp mission director, and all-around responsible and good person. I had answers before people asked the questions. I was not afraid to give advice and to take the wheel when necessary (or available). Life was a meaningful adventure. Yes, of course, there was pain, but for the most part, I had it figured out: the narrative was clear, the map accurate, my nest secure. God was leading me, and I was on the right path, among people who had "cracked the code" to a life of, if not reward and punishment, then unconditional love and natural consequences.

God was the foolproof strength in my corner, the One who'd never let me down. And my family was the first and most important place this message was reinforced. Dad-Pastor-God images were happily comingled, and so were Home-Church-Family images. My family was the epicenter of strength and identity—not just for me but for the many others who read my dad's books and watched us. And I knew they were watching: we were living proof of my dad's teachings on display. We had an invincible family to go with our invincible faith. We knew that we were exceptional and that we had to use our powers for good. To sum up: God was love, I was beloved, church was fun and warm and the seat of all truth, and I belonged unequivocally. Life was good. I was safe, maybe even invincible.

I hadn't much occasion in my life to confront Jesus's question, *Who do you say that I am?* Or, for that matter, to wrestle too seriously with my own, *Who am I?* to any real and soul-shaking degree. Both questions were already answered quite satisfactorily for me. I hadn't yet learned what *Messiah* really meant or what being human was really about. The suffering I experienced was bearable, understandable; it fit into the simple "God, obedience, love, and consequences" framework of things. And where it didn't, the framework expanded slightly to include it—which is to say, it bent but didn't break. I believed equally in Christian slogans like "God can't give you more than you can handle" and upbeat interpretations of Scripture passages such as "All things work together for good for those who love God" (Rom 8:28).

There is nothing especially wrong with this kind of faith. And as long as life doesn't throw you a curveball, it's possible to claim it for a very long time and to have a very happy life within this framework. But when things fall apart, when *Who am I?* and *Who is God?* bulldoze their way onto the scene, something must die in order for a new experience of God to break in. And when that happens, what it means to be human, and to be church, gets radically redefined.

Youth group was the pinnacle toward which all church childhood was striving. Whitewater rafting, Nerd Night, winter skiing, short-term mission trips to Haiti, and fall retreats: after God spoke the world into being, it wasn't until our church youth group that life was perfected. Every week started with more than a hundred teenagers belting out the theme song from *Cheers*, about how hard life is, and needing a break from worries, and how we all want to be "where everybody knows your name (dum, dee, dee, dee, dee, dum, dum!)."

It was with the youth group that I left the country for the first time, as the first person in my family to do so. At fourteen, I spent two weeks helping to run a vacation Bible school for kids in a ramshackle church sanctuary in Saint-Marc, Haiti, sleeping under a mosquito net on the floor of a house with twenty-five other teenagers. I tasted goat-brain soup, rode through a swollen river in the back of a huge flatbed truck, and washed my body with baby wipes. (The rainstorm on the second Monday was the only time we'd wash our hair.) That trip awoke in me a fire for travel and for learning about other cultures that has endured to this day. It also set me apart in school: "Oh, you're part of *that* youth group."

Our leaders—the senior-high pastor, two associate pastors, and a handful of volunteers—were woven into our lives. They attended our sports games, visited us at our first jobs, and dropped in to have lunch with us at school. We hung out at their houses for barbecues or movie nights. We were the animated eyewitnesses to a marriage proposal between two of them, and we made up a good chunk of the congregation at their wedding. Our youth leaders were the ones we turned to with blossoming crushes, problems in school, and struggles with anxiety.

My junior year, the senior-high youth pastor moved into the newly created "missions pastor" post. All those youth trips had kindled in him a longing to shepherd groups of people into God's world full time, and this job shift meant he could do that, not just with youth, but with adult groups as well in our congregation of more than five thousand people.

When a new head youth pastor was hired, things changed abruptly. He brought with him a programmatic framework and a cadre of enthusiastic volunteers he'd recruited from his own former youth group in Chicago and from a local Bible college. We stopped singing the *Cheers* song. Instead of inviting us to his house for a barbecue or sharing about his own struggles, he taught an entire Bible-study lesson, prayed for us, and sent us home—one time without telling us his mother had died that very day. He presented a faith that was certain and strong and kept his pain a secret.

The other youth staff and volunteers were let go or gradually left. We went from regularly connecting with easily six to ten adults whom we deeply trusted to interacting with the same number of strangers, nearly overnight. The events that shaped the rhythm of our lives, which we'd come to anticipate and rely on year after year, were canceled, and in their place were unfamiliar conferences and get-to-know-you mixers.

One night I arrived at our beloved youth room in the huge former high school building where our congregation made its home to discover the worn couches, foosball tables, and poster-sized photos of us in various states of hilarity that had filled the walls replaced with preschool toys, rocking chairs, and baby swings. Our youth room had been commandeered for the nursery expansion. I was directed to drive to the "old building," a mile and a half away, which housed the church offices. When I arrived in the dark parking lot and made my way to the wide-open former sanctuary space, cheerful strangers at the door warmly welcomed me to the church I had been part of since I was three years old and handed me a visitor card.

Several months later, our associate youth pastor, the last remaining adult many of us had known as "pastor"—someone we could go to, who knew and loved us—was fired. By this point, instead of the hundred kids who consistently gathered, only perhaps eight to ten senior-high youth were attending on Wednesday nights, and half of them were new. We were nearly all struggling with the sudden loss of support, not to mention the vacuum created by the loss of the social center the youth group had been for all of us for so long. In fear and worry, I watched the alarmingly rapid downward spiral of my youth-group friends, whose struggles included drug use, eating disorders, mental illness, domestic violence, and at least one pregnancy. We felt we had nowhere to turn. We felt sad, scared, and alone.

One evening, a group of thirty youth gathered in the living room of one kid's home to figure out what to do. We'd been raised to be brave and tell the truth, to trust our leaders and ask for help, and so we did. The congregation was enormous; perhaps the elders just were not aware of what was happening to the youth group. We were their kids. They loved us and had a wonderful plan for our lives. They would help us.

At sixteen, I was the leader of the resistance, drafter of The Letter, and I was sent with three other high school representatives to bring our concerns to the church board. We were nervous and eager to share. All the kids were counting on us. The board welcomed us kindly and listened with concern. We left feeling hopeful and relieved. But rumors spread fast. When the story of our visit to the board took shape, the new version was that we were trying to get the new youth pastor fired.

I heard myself referred to by adults I had known and trusted my whole life as "spoiled," "unwilling to accept change," "undermining," and "sneaky." Our parents (some of them, like my own, pastors or board members) stood by us. Other staff leaders condemned us. I lost my church babysitting jobs and volunteer gigs, and many adults would no longer look me in the eye over donut holes after Sunday services. The ensuing drama nearly split the entire church.[1]

We remaining high school kids came to be seen as a risky investment at best, malicious more likely. Deciding to pour its resources and attention into the younger age groups, the church had chosen, according to one leader, to "grow a new youth group rather than pursue the batch of bad apples that had rotted off the tree." The new senior-high pastor resigned, and the church leaders decided to bank on the robust junior-high group and not to provide staff or create programming for the senior-high group for a few years. There were hardly any kids left anyway.

Confused, deeply hurt, feeling betrayed and abandoned, most of my peers soured on Christianity altogether, and many have not returned to church since. I was labeled dangerous and dismissed by the authority figures whose approval had so fed and shaped me. A few of us kids scraped together gatherings, recruited parent volunteers, and sought to rebuild, or at least preserve a remnant of, our youth group, but none of the original kids remained.

That summer I learned that while everything else had been canceled, our annual spot at a local camp for the fall retreat had been overlooked. We could use it if we wanted to. I gathered some kids and former volunteers, and we organized the event. Ninety youth showed up. We called it "The Band-Aid Retreat." For two days, kids who hadn't seen each other in months shared their stories. It was visceral and genuine, and for the first time in my memory of youth group, we prayed for one another. After that retreat, we all scattered back into our lives, and at seventeen, I found myself teetering on the edge of ministry burnout, feeling hurt, confused, and disillusioned about what church was or should be. *What is church?*

Not long afterward, I graduated from high school and immediately spent five months in a discipleship training school ive months in a discipleship training school (DTS), an extended, live-in Bible study and service project on a hospital ship off the coast of Senegal. This was a chance to travel and see the world, to leave behind disillusion and exhaustion, and to experience God and my life in a completely different way.

Psalm 107 tells us that God redeems in any and all circumstances; God's love endures forever. It's a lovely, poetic collection of stories of people in various kinds of trouble and God's salvation of them. As it goes through stories of God's redemption, the psalm is specific; salvation comes in exactly the form that each group mentioned needs. The psalm tells of those who were lost, alone, helpless, who had reached the end of their capacity to adapt or cope, and how they cried out to God—and God delivered, God redeemed.

> Some wandered in desert wastes,
>> finding no way to an inhabited town;
> hungry and thirsty,
>> their soul fainted within them. . . .

They cried to the Lord in their trouble,
    and he delivered them from their distress;
he led them by a straight way,
    until they reached an inhabited town. . . .

Some sat in darkness and in gloom,
    prisoners in misery and in irons. . . .
They cried to the Lord in their trouble,
    and he saved them from their distress;
he brought them out of darkness and gloom,
    and broke their bonds asunder. . . .

Some went down to the sea in ships,
    doing business on the mighty waters. . . .
They mounted up to heaven, they went down to the
    depths;
    their courage melted away in their calamity;
they reeled and staggered like drunkards,
    and were at their wits' end. . . .
They cried to the Lord in their trouble,
    And he brought them out from their distress;
he made the storm be still,
    and the waves of the sea were hushed.

Salvation comes as deliverance from what is holding us captive, wholeness where we are broken, direction where we are lost, and connection where we are severed. It comes as hope in despair and new beginnings after bitter endings. As this psalm illustrates, the salvation of God always brings to us just what will heal us—even if it isn't necessarily what we think it should be—because salvation is always about restoring us to our true connection to God and each other. It doesn't mean dead people come back (yet), fortunes are reversed, the world is suddenly fair, or pain we've caused can be taken back and erased. But it means the way forward in Christ is deep and true connection to God and each other. Connection to God and each other is our beginning and our end, our origin and our destiny.

A small group of girls had been meeting regularly at the home of a family friend, Jenny. Jenny had three boys to my family's four girls, and our families loved to share meals, outings, and weekend trips. Where my own mom was outgoing, loud, funny, a little invasive, and a lot disorganized, Jenny was gentle and orderly, soft-spoken and tidy. They were good friends; Jenny was yin to my mom's yang. Apart from my parents, Jenny was the adult who most stood by me and supported me through the youth-group scandal.

On the day before I was to leave for Senegal, Jenny said goodbye to me from her bed, where she was resting, felled by a bad case of bronchitis turned to pneumonia. She didn't want to hug me for fear of spreading her germs, but she handed me a gift. I peeled off the wrapping paper to reveal a day planner with a message, Bible verse, or prayer for every day of the six months I would be away. Jenny had solicited friends and family to fill the pages with words of support and love. Many of them were penned in her own hand. "I'm so excited to see what God does in your life, Kara," she rasped. "Have a wonderful time!"

I arrived in Dakar tired and disoriented, yearning for new life, adventure, and renewed faith, needing to forgive, and needing to seek forgiveness. I found myself in a community of persistent healing and practiced trust. I was far from home, living temporarily alongside people who had given up everything ordinary in life to move onto a hospital ship and serve others. Doctors and nurses, mechanics and schoolteachers made up an international floating society, united in belief and purpose. I was inspired and humbled. God was visible, faith was tangible, and I felt so alive and grateful to be there.

The first few weeks I was on the ship, I fell into a rhythm. I would begin my day exactly three minutes before class started. After rolling out of bed and throwing on a shirt and skirt, pulling my hair into a ponytail, and brushing my teeth, I would race upstairs to find my seat in the classroom near the window above the ship's gangplank. In the wake of this whirlwind, I'd leave my pajamas hanging from my bunk ladder and my bright green sleeping bag printed with glow-in-the-dark Jersey cows tangled on my top bunk—the first thing you'd see when you entered our berth. The tidy cubbies and hospital corners of my German, Norwegian, and Swedish roommates' beds in our tiny cabin couldn't make up for my colorful and aggressive overspill.

Once I was in the classroom, the warm breeze would come through the porthole next to me, and I would see three things below me every morning. First, I would see the mission's construction crews loading trucks with supplies and equipment before they headed out to the remote site where a clinic was being built and I'd watch the mobile clinic teams leave in vans for various pop-up locations.

Second, I would see two lines of people—a longer line, already formed, of those seeking care and a shorter line of people awaiting surgery. The longer line stretched from a tent with chairs and tables set up across the street from the ship's entrance and reached all the way down the block; the shorter line started at the bottom of the gangplank and pressed against the side of the ship. Both lines included many children with visible deformities—mostly cleft lip and palate or cataract blindness but also children and adults with twisted or missing limbs or burn scars and some with no external signs of ailment but with tumors or other hidden diseases.

And third, I would see the ship's doors open and a few nurses and doctors stride down the gangplank with clipboards, stethoscopes, and boxes to set up shop in the tent, attending to and screening those in the long line who were hoping to receive help.

Then one nurse would make her way down the gangplank to welcome the first family group in the short line and escort them up the gangplank into the ship. I knew that while I sat in class, the family would sit waiting somewhere comfortable in the belly of the ship while their child was wheeled into a surgery room and that before lunch the whole trajectory of the child's life would be changed.

In the evenings after our work was finished, we would hear stories of small and big miracles, of lives altered in the hull of the ship or in the remote clinics. We would hear the families rejoicing, the children tucked into beds in recovery rooms, ready to go home to their villages or back to school or play in the streets of the city where they would be able to see, or speak, for the first time. Their lives would no longer be shaped primarily by their affliction—living as outcasts, enduring shunning, without opportunity or hope for change. And together each night we celebrated and thanked God for healing them, for being able to share in their stories, for God's faithfulness and love, God's salvation in their lives. *Give thanks to the Lord! God's faithfulness endures forever!*

A few weeks into this routine, I heard my name called over the ship loudspeaker in the Australian accent of the receptionist, with "Please report to reception; you have a phone call." The ship was docked in Senegal, and calls were six dollars per minute. I'd heard from my parents only by fax. I picked up the receiver. "Hello?"

"Kara, it's Jenny! How are you, honey?"

"Hi, Jenny! I'm good!" I answered. It was so good to hear her voice, but I was confused about why she was calling me.

"I know this has to be quick, Kara, but I wanted to tell you myself and not write it in a fax. I'm calling to tell you that I don't have pneumonia. It turns out that what I have is stage 4 lung cancer. Honey, I am going to fight it. I have faith that I will be healed. Please pray for me. We are going to beat this."

I hung up and stumbled back to my cabin. There, from my ship bunk in the heat of the Port of Dakar, I launched an aggressive, tireless campaign of fervent prayer and fasting. I absolutely trusted God to come through, as I'd always known he would in times of great need. I'd been trained for this! Claiming the power of Jesus to heal, rebuking sickness and death, I pleaded with the Almighty to accept my fasting and prayers and heal my friend. I knew how this battle worked. I too had faith.

But after a couple of weeks, I was depleted entirely. Jenny was deteriorating rapidly, and I had come to the end of myself. Ashamed and confused, I admitted defeat.

Then, in the spent emptiness of sorrow and despair, I felt God speak to me.

Am I still the Healer, Kara, even if I don't heal Jenny?

Who is God?

All around me I was witnessing God's healing. Families singing and dancing on the docks beneath my porthole as they welcomed back a loved one, healed. The mobile clinic teams returning with stories of redemption and hope shared at nightly gatherings. And in this community of love and presence, my own heart had begun to mend. I had found a way to forgive, to let go, to take responsibility for my part in what had happened with the youth group, and to seek reconciliation. Even in the panic and the anguish of knowing my friend was dying, and feeling utterly helpless and desperate, I was watching new life open up all around—and even within—me. God could heal! Why not her? I didn't understand it. But I also couldn't deny it.

I felt myself enter into the paradox. In the stillness, I answered back: *Yes. Yes, God. You are the Healer, no matter what.*

For the next five months, my life was a juxtaposition of two realities. On the one hand, my dear friend was rapidly dying a senseless and terrible death, which no amount of medical intervention or fervent prayers slowed or stopped. And on the other hand, I daily witnessed miracles—both those helped by medicine and those that came about through prayer alone. My "ask and you shall receive," easy trust in the God of guarantees eroded and vanished. I was forced to reckon with a God who was God of both situations.

In the evenings we gathered—four hundred people from forty countries living together on that ship. We prayed for the sick, we praised God for God's faithfulness and love, and we witnessed God's salvation time and again. Wells were dug and clinics built, prayers were answered and people were healed, relationships were formed, communities were strengthened, and the name of Jesus was lifted high.

But back home Jenny was surrounded too. People sang to her, held her hand, cared for her children and her husband, wept and raged and resigned themselves, and prayed and held one another as she slipped away. And so, in both gatherings, one on the deck of a ship in the Port of Dakar and another in a hospital room in Minneapolis, one in joy and another in suffering, stories were told, people cried out to God, and the Lord was thanked for steadfast love.

Years later, when I served as a hospital chaplain, I witnessed how, faced with sudden tragedy or prolonged suffering, people would either tell the truth of their circumstances and cry out in their distress or praise and give thanks to God. Only rarely did I meet a person who could do both. We seem to believe that to trust God requires that we deny or reframe suffering and loss, that we minimize it so as not to diminish God's greatness or worthiness to receive our gratitude. Conversely, we seem to think that in order to give thanks to God or recognize God's faithfulness, we can't be truthful about how terrible our suffering is.

But suspended between these two realities, I discovered this: in the face of great suffering, we call out to God. As creatures of our Creator, it's what we do. It's what we are meant to do. We can speak out the reality of our situation, and we can cry out to God in our trouble. That is *our* action, *our* participation. The work of salvation—delivering, healing, restoring—is God's work. We cannot do that; only God can.

We can tell the story of our need and ask God to intervene, ask God to help us. And we can thank God, remember what God has done, speak it out, recount to each other and to the world God's faithfulness, God's steadfast love. This is the way we find salvation—salvation that comes right to our places of need. We cry out to God in distress, and we thank God for God's steadfast love. Both of these, together. They are both true; both lament and praise tell the truth about who God is, who we are, and the reality we are living in right now.

The practice of faith, faithing, isn't believing in an invincible God or clinging to certain ideals. It's more a practice with two movements: speaking our reality by crying out to God for help and remembering God's faithfulness by thanking God. In this relationship with the Divine, whom we don't own and can't control, we must be who we are, in whatever situation we are in, truthfully. And we must allow God to be who God is, however God chooses to reveal Godself to us.

This faithing happens in community, not alone. Though certainly God meets us in solitude, our lament and worship are essential communal expressions of our humanity. We need others to bear them with us, and we are made to bear these with and for others. Even when we are alone—even grieving or praising alone—our lives are bound up with others, and we do not bear our grief or our celebration in isolation. We experience God's steadfast love in and through others, and we share it with others. When we are with and for each other, we meet Jesus who is with and for us. So, when one cries out in need, we all carry that cry, and when one celebrates the deliverance of God, we all thank God together. In Christ we gather; in Christ, we find our story. God is not apart from us, but in Christ, God is the One who suffered death, was raised to life, and promises life to come.

Held within this diverse and faith-filled community, I both cried out to God in my distress and expressed gratitude for God's salvation and love, *at the same time*. And in the midst of this intense juxtaposition, my relationship with God changed. It grew more complex, more nuanced, less simple. Faith was less straightforward. Trust shifted from easy to complicated. It stopped depending on my feeling good, or getting what I want, or ask for, or think is best in the world, and it looked instead to the character and being of the Divine, who is with and for us in all things.

Two months later, from a campground in the Canary Islands, where we were taking a day off from our mission outreach routine of performing street theater with altar calls, I received another long-distance phone call. My team leader came to get me from the swimming pool.

Shivering in my swimsuit and towel, and dripping all over the concrete floor of the campground office, I took the phone and heard the voice I loved whisper the words I dreaded. "Kara, I don't have much longer. I want to tell you I love you. And no matter what, hang on to Jesus."

"I love you too, Jenny," I said.

"I won't let you say goodbye; this is not goodbye. We will see each other again one day, Kara. It will be just a little longer than we had planned. Maybe we just say, 'See you later.'"

The air in the office was suddenly suffocating. I couldn't breathe. Sorrow and pain clawed up my throat and were cut off when she forbade me from saying what I most wanted to say, *Goodbye. Why couldn't I tell her goodbye?*

So instead, through tears and in a voice I tried to steady for her sake, I stammered an awkward "Bon voyage."

"See you later, Kara."

Those were the last words she spoke to me. Shortly after that, Jenny stopped speaking altogether. My family and friends were gathered around her bedside when the machines and the medications were all that kept her alive. And when they were removed and she breathed her last breath, they were there, by her side. And I was sitting on a bus on a dirt road somewhere between Senegal and the Gambia in the afternoon heat far, far away. Jenny died in her thirties, with three children under ten years old.

God's steadfast love endures—in life and in death, forever. And God continues to meet us with exactly the salvation we need, to save us in the midst of—if not from—our troubles.[2] One way God's salvation reached me in the midst of my grief was through Jenny's own words. After she died, as my time in Africa and Europe neared its end, I still encountered messages from Jenny in my day-planner; she still had words for me. I'd open the book in the morning and turn the page to that day's date and see her words to me: "Kara, you must be learning and experiencing so much! It's amazing how God works in our lives. I love you and miss you!—Jenny." Or,

"Kara, God is so faithful! May you remember today how much Jesus loves you.—Jenny."

I would trace the letters with my finger and imagine her writing them there as I prepared to set out on my healing adventure, a lifetime ago. Her love continued to speak to me, even after she was united completely with Love itself. If my experience were made a stanza in Psalm 107, it might go like this:

Some were far away
> while the life of a dear friend was stolen early
>> by a terrible cancer.

They heard of the suffering but could not be near;
> their grief was overwhelming,
> and they could make no sense of it.

Then they cried out to God in their trouble,
> and he delivered them from their distress:

God drew near to them in their sorrow
> and gave peace in the midst of the pain.

God gave them precious words to share
> and stories of healing, hope, and redemption,
> happening to others in their very midst,

and God surrounded them with love and support.

Let them thank the Lord for his steadfast love,
> For God's wonderful works to humankind.

For God holds us from eternity to eternity,
> sustains us by God's Spirit,
> and in life and death we belong to Christ.

—Psalm 107, my own stanza

Though we'd likely never agree with this truth in the midst of the experience, disillusionment is ultimately a gift. It frees us from illusions. In order for new life to come, something has to die. Often the death of illusion comes with the death of someone we love, the death of a dream, or the loss of something we've depended on all our life. The false crumbles, and only then can the real be discovered. I had seen behind the curtain. Church wasn't Oz, and God wasn't the wizard. Prayer isn't a vending-machine transaction, and faith isn't a guaranteed strategy for manipulating the Divine to get what we want. God is free. Free to heal, and free not to. And I don't get to understand why. Nevertheless, God is the Healer. God is with us. God is trustworthy.

After his diagnosis, Marty jumped into chemotherapy, and we jumped with him. People drove him to appointments and made him meals. Despite feeling very ill, he stayed generally upbeat and optimistic. He adapted to the fight, putting his retirement plans on hold to tackle this thing first. For now, Marty was focused on the task at hand: get through chemo. Survive the agony of this day, then the next. What comes after, and the big picture, would have to wait. This all would be just another hurdle, another challenge, something else to put in his life resume—which was more colorful and eclectic than we yet knew.

Will you allow us to be, for you and with you, the body of Christ in love and service, joy and suffering, sharing life and faith together?

we had asked him when he became a member. And he'd answered, "I will." So we were making good on our promise, and he was making good on his. If this was where he was going, we were going there with him, because we were church together. He might be sad, he may be scared, but he was not alone. Because this is where God was, where God always is.

Chapter 3

When We Pay Attention and Join In

———◆———

Our capacity for the transcendent is precisely what distinguishes us most from the rest of visible creation. It is what makes us most human.

—THOMAS KEATING, *Heart of the World*

The Church is the Church only when it exists for others.

—DIETRICH BONHOEFFER,
Letters and Papers from Prison

March 2016

*I*n the beginning of March 2016, a thinner and completely bald Marty walked into my office and sat down in the overstuffed chair facing me on the couch. He didn't take off his jacket. His face was pinched in worry, his shoulders hunched forward in anxiety, his hands gripping the arms of the chair tightly. He looked scared. He looked defeated.

A couple of months had passed since his diagnosis. In that time, chemotherapy meant that Marty had lost his hair and his appetite. He was miserable but did his best not to show it. The cancer was more widespread than doctors initially thought—having begun, he learned, with a tumor behind his knee that spread to his spine and his brain, peppering his lungs with tumors. The lump behind his knee was now protruding enough to be felt, and being able to lean down and touch the cancer made it all the more real and horrifying for him. He was hanging on for follow-up tests to determine whether the chemo was working. For the past nine weeks, his life had been oriented toward this goal: get through the chemo; get the updated test results. Finally, the time had come, and his follow-up tests were done.

"Thanks for meeting with me, Kara," he said. Without hesitation or pleasantries, he plunged in, his stutter making what he had come to say take longer to come out. "I just don't know what to do! The chemo isn't working. It hasn't shrunk the tumors at all. The doctor wants to do another kind of chemo that has even less success with my kind of cancer. But I have been so sick from the treatment, and I just don't want to go through that. I won't."

"Oh, Marty, I am so sorry," I replied, my heart squeezing in my chest and my eyes filling with tears. This felt unimaginable. I was watching him try to tell me that he was choosing not to fight it. That he was going to accept his own impending death. How does someone say something like that to another person? He just does. He just says it. Saying it can make it more real, and in saying it to someone else, he was also saying it to himself.

He cried for a few minutes. His shoulders shook. I gave him a tissue and sat, silent. Then he settled into his seat, raised his face back to me, and continued.

"They don't know for sure, but they think I have maybe six weeks . . . ? To be honest, Kara, I am afraid. I am really scared. I don't know how to do this. I don't know how to do all the things . . . find hospice, how to go through all this . . . alone."

I took a breath and took him in. Then I took his hand and said what I knew to be true. "First of all," I answered, "you are not alone. There are at least thirty people right now who will drive you to appointments, bring you food, help you figure out hospice. You're not alone, Marty. You have us."

The tension left him, and his shoulders dropped. I could hear the relief in his voice. "Oh, thank you, Kara. That really means a lot to me."

I let go of his hand and looked right in his eyes, as I felt something dawn on me. "But also, Marty," I blurted, "you are out ahead of us, going where we are *all* going. You're on a journey every single one of us will be taking at some point. Would you be willing to let us share this with you?"

Marty's whole demeanor transformed before my eyes. He suddenly sat taller in his seat. His shoulders squared. His hands fell into his lap. His face softened for a moment, and then it positively lit up. With wonder in his voice, he said, "Kara, you make me feel like I have a calling!"

"Oh, Marty!" I replied, awed by the visible shift in him. "I think it *is* a calling!" I smiled. "Could we commission you to it? Would you let us lay hands on you and name that calling?"

"Yes. I would like that. I'd like that very much," he responded.

We meet Jesus, who is with and for us when we are with and for each other. We say these words a lot in our church, but these are not just words. We say it because it's true. Christ is concretely present when we bear each other's burdens and share each other's joy. When we are near to each other in our suffering and joy, we are near to Jesus. When we share life with each other, we are sharing life with Jesus. I know this to be true.

There isn't a way to premeditate this. There's no manual for ministry. I mean, there are thousands of manuals, actually, but in the end, the only way to do it is *to do it*. To be *you*, alongside *them*, in *it*, whatever *it* is. In this way, it's like parenting. All the books and advice in the world are not what you need in the moment. You need to *be* there, to be *present* with your child, in this unique space, defined by whatever it is that you are sharing at this moment.

There was no pastoral training or preparation that could give me the right thing to say or do when someone is sitting across from me telling me they're trying to get their head around the appalling fact that they're going to die very soon. In that moment with Marty, I only knew that we belonged to each other, and that meant we were with and for each other in this. He might be sad, he may be scared, but he was not alone.

I was with him. We were with him. God was here. All I could do, *what* I could do, was to be here with him.

What that meant in practical terms was that I could let myself feel the pain and horror of Marty's too-soon death too. I could cry with him and trust that Christ was with us then. I could trust that by letting myself be fully present in this moment with this person, I was where Jesus was. I could trust that I would be given what I needed to minister to Marty, that the Holy Spirit would give me whatever I would need to share in whatever God was doing in that moment.

In the middle of my liberal arts education at a small, Christian college, I received a panicked email from a friend of mine, Dana, in South Carolina:

> kara . . . i really need to get some biblical guidance. . . .
> i have a dear friend, mollie, who has become a jaded
> baptist and is seriously considering mormonism. . . .
> i dont know what to say anymore. . . . i certainly
> am not trained like those missionaries they have to
> defend my faith . . .

She ended,

> whatever insight you can provide would be greatly
> appreciated and if that is nothing . . . that's superfly
> okay too. . . . take care.
>
> djc

My pulse raced and my fingers itched to write back. My oldest-child, faith-trained self kicked into gear. I wrote back affirming her worry and offering a confident list of books "exposing" the dangers of Mormonism. But then I added some questions she might ask Mollie: What is she really looking for? What about Mormonism looks so attractive? Does it seem to fit what she needs, or is it the only thing she sees that seems better than what she has now? I suggested that Mollie should keep searching, set this time aside for her and God, and not decide too quickly and end up stuck in something else that was no better than what she left.

After a while, I heard that Mollie had gone through with it. She had become Mormon and that was the end of it. But five months later I received an email from Mollie herself.

She then told me that she had printed the questions I'd written and carried them with her, intending to write at some point, but life got too crazy. And now, while she felt great about her decision to join the Church of Jesus Christ of Latter-day Saints and had no doubts that it was the right decision, she did not feel great about her relationship with Dana and the toll her choice had taken on their friendship. She asked if I had any advice about staying connected with Dana.

This opened up a daily email conversation that spanned many months. These were the days when we mostly had to go to the campus computer lab to send email, and Mollie in South Carolina and I in Minnesota spent much of the next few months hunkered in our college computer labs. My first response to Mollie was simply about Dana. I reserved any opinion about the rest of her message and just tried to address what she was asking me. But within a few days, she was pouring out her story in a single message that stretched over several sittings.

She shared about her process, and the deep longing she had for God and for truth, and all the things in her life leading up to her own decision to convert. The more Mollie told me about her experience and her search, the less certain I felt in my own rightness and opinion about her life. It was disconcerting.

Mollie had been disillusioned and sickened by the hypocrisy in her experience of church for a long time. She and her college classmates would show up Sunday morning in the pews next to their parents to pray and sing, sickened with hangovers and shame from a weekend of wild partying. *What does religion or faith even mean to me?* she'd wonder. She longed to please God; more than anything, this was the driving force of her life.

When she looked around her, the people who seemed to be most committed, most devoted to God, with the strongest sense of integrity, were the Mormons. No matter where she looked, she told me, Mormons everywhere looked the same. Their lives matched their beliefs. They seemed so faithful and committed to God. So she had started exploring their faith. And after a long-drawn-out, prayer-filled, deeply researched process, Mollie eventually made the decision to convert.

> i spent a lot of time praying about what to do. i hope
> you realize that i really only want what is pleas-
> ing to God, because after all what could be more

> important? i spent a lot of time praying and read-
> ing literature, both from the church and against the
> church. i really do believe that i received an answer
> from God that the mormon church is Christ's true
> church.

She said the hardest thing was telling her parents. They were
devastated, angry, ashamed of her.

> it was as if i crushed their whole world. it also hurt
> me because i know how disappointed in me they
> were. it's so ironic that the time they're most disap-
> pointed in me is the time when i'm trying my hard-
> est in life to do the right thing. Yet, when i was living
> in so much sin, they couldn't have been happier
> because at least I was baptist.

When I read that, I sat back with a start, my breath catching in my chest. I realized that I had been feeling *the same way*.
Not as dramatically as her parents, obviously. I had nothing
invested in her faith life personally; I hardly knew this person. But I knew, or at least I thought I did, how faith in Christ
worked, and I had a lot invested in those beliefs. This story
was not fitting my template. I'd been seeing Mollie's decision
in the same way her parents and friends were—as a choice to
move *away* from truth, *away* from God.

But I also believed the Bible, when Jesus said, "Ask, and
it will be given you; search, and you will find; knock, and the
door will be opened for you. For everyone who asks receives,
and everyone who searches finds, and for everyone who

knocks, the door will be opened" (Matt 7:7–8). "When you search for me, you will find me; if you seek me with all your heart" (Jer 29:13). And I had never seen anyone seek God with their whole heart with the absolute fervency and dedication that I was witnessing in Mollie.

And so I was stuck.

If I were going to be in a conversation with Mollie about her life, I would have to give up my own ideas about what her life should look like. This was a brand-new thought for me. Wasn't having opinions about what other people's lives should look like intrinsic to Christianity? Suddenly, I felt myself at a crossroads. Which direction would be the stronger pull: my belief about what Mollie's life *should* look like? Or the honesty of her longing for God and the trustworthiness of God's promise in Scripture?

When I asked myself these questions this starkly, there was no contest. It was clear to me that in order to truly accompany Mollie on her journey, I would have to give up my own ideas about what her faith *should* look like, where she *should* ultimately "arrive." When God says, "When you seek me, you will find me," this is real. It will really happen. Or did I not believe that? I'd learned that God is free to be who God is and to reveal Godself how God will. So who was I to claim to know better than God? And who was I to claim to know better than Mollie about her own life? Could I allow that her own seeking was a beautiful and brave form of obedience—already moving in a God-directed way?

I felt God asking me, *Are you willing to trust me with Mollie? Will you trust that I am leading her? That I won't abandon her?* It was not unlike the question I had been asked by the Divine back in

Senegal, as I prayed for Jenny to be healed. *Am I the Healer, Kara, even if I don't heal Jenny?* Would I trust that God is God, even if the outcome looks different than I think it should? Could I separate myself and my agenda from the presence and work of God in someone's life? And then the invitation: Did I want to be along for this kind of a ride? Specifically, could I get out of the way of what God might be doing in Mollie's life? If so, I would be permitted to accompany her. If not, I might as well stand with her parents in saying we'd all rather she be a back-slidden Baptist than a faithful Mormon.

Who is God? Can God be trusted?

For the next several months, we wrote back and forth about her conversion experience and her burgeoning life as a Mormon and about my own faith and experiences of God. Mollie and I wrestled through Bible passages, church doctrines, and theological conceptions of faith, grace, salvation, and more. We shared the mundane parts of our days and our deep questions and struggles. For the first couple of weeks, we were cautious, always worried about offending each other. Then we set that aside and said, *Let's just be honest.* Throughout this time, I continually prayed for the strength to stay open to her journey and to be able to see God leading her.

We'd come to know each other's "voice" in print so well. But the first time we spoke on the phone, Mollie's thick Southern accent and my distinct Minnesota inflection made conversation nearly impossible. We could barely understand each other, and we mostly laughed.

The deeper Mollie delved into her new faith, the more questions came up for her, and we wrote about those too.

I learned how to hold her questions with her, to ask back to her, *What was that like? How does that strike you?* She began to grieve that, contrary to first impressions, people are people everywhere. Hypocrisy and division are universally shared sins that nobody escapes. Perhaps this system of beliefs and practices had looked more authentic from a distance simply because the list of rules was longer, the demands to conform stronger, and the defining characteristics of belonging to this group were clearer, so it took longer to notice the duplicity and inconsistencies. At its core, the Mormon Church was just another institution. She had really just switched out one system of beliefs for another. It wasn't going to save her. And it didn't get her any closer to what she was craving.

What Mollie most wanted was to know and feel her connection to God. She wanted to live in union with Christ and others. She wanted to know, *Who is God? Who am I? How should I live my life?* What Mollie really longed for deeply was Jesus. Jesus isn't owned by one institution or denomination, or even one religion, for that matter. Jesus is God with us. Jesus is with and for us, right here and now; God who won't let us go, no matter what.

Being a disciple is not a set of beliefs or a system of religion. It's "a state of being," as Rowan Williams says so beautifully in *Being Disciples*. It's a state of *attentive expectancy*, watching for God, listening for God, readiness to be called into the action of God. And this can begin wherever you are, at any and every moment.

Our emails started shifting. We began to notice clear divisions between the structures and beliefs of various expressions of religion, and a relationship with a living God, the presence of God with us, and the love of Christ in all the ways Christ encounters us. How was God meeting her even right now? A few months in, she wrote,

> kara, i have come to realize a lot of things. my whole life I have tried to find God in so many ways, so many resources. And that is exactly what i am still trying to do with the mormon church and with looking to another church for answers. it's almost like I just have to have something concrete so i can observe it and know that it is real. but what does that say about faith? . . . i don't mean that i don't believe in God because i can't see him. i just mean that a relationship with God is not as concrete as a church. you know?
>
> and kara, i've looked for god so long in everything that I almost don't even know how to look just to Him. either that or it is just second nature for me to turn to other things. i know that i can change it but right now this is almost more "comfortable." i hope that doesn't sound blasphemous or some-thing. i do want to find Him more than anything but I almost don't know how to just look at the source and not the resource. and none of the resources can provide what it is i'm looking for so i keep coming up empty. And kara, it is not even that i am doing this and don't realize it, because i do. it is just such a learned and instilled behavior.

It's hard to overstate, in hindsight, what kind of education this was for me—both in the near-constant invitation to study and wrestle with and share Mollie's questions without imposing my own agenda and to keep paying attention with expectancy to my own life and faith. Because she was seeking, so was I. Because she was watching for God, so was I. I didn't know where this would lead for her, but it no longer mattered all that much. I knew *who* was leading us, and my trust in God continued to increase.

The first time we met in person, we had no idea what each other looked like. In an airport, a short, smiling person approached me, and Mollie, in her now familiar Southern drawl, said, "Kara? Is that you?" We hugged and laughed and cried and spent our visit staying up late talking about God.

I was all set to go to grad school for a PhD in psychology at Fuller Theological Seminary, a school that offered an additional master's degree in theology woven into the psychology program. One of my final college courses was on serious psychological disorders, such as schizophrenia, bipolar disorder, and clinical depression. Halfway through the class, I imagined myself sitting in an office, day after day, dealing with mental illness or digging into childhood trauma, filling out reams of paperwork, and following up on treatment plans. That wasn't what I really wanted. What I wanted was more of what was happening right then with Mollie. I wanted to accompany people in their own reflection on their lives and together to listen for what God might be doing. I wasn't sure what to do next, but I knew I was *not* meant to be a licensed psychologist.

One afternoon, shortly before graduation but after I'd changed my mind about being a psychologist, I was flipping wistfully through Fuller's catalog. In the middle of a page of concentrations for theology degrees was a small paragraph about something called "spiritual direction." I had never heard of this. But right in front of me, in black and white, was a description of *exactly* what had been happening between Mollie and me. "Spiritual Direction is the process of accompanying someone in their faith life, discerning along with them the presence and activity of God." I got goose bumps and immediately applied for this program. I was absolutely certain it was where I was meant to be.

In the meantime, Mollie had navigated through so much upheaval, personal awakening, and spiritual deepening. She was attending both the Mormon Church and a little nondenominational congregation in her town. The tension in the social situations between her competing groups of friends was extreme. She was simultaneously living with one foot in each of two vastly different worlds. But her own inner life and connection with God were integrating and settling. All the fear about pleasing God and not letting God down had begun to dissipate, and in its place was a growing sense of trust as she tried placing her own life, and people she cared about, in God's hands.

And then something broke open. At some point, her striving just stopped. Something clicked into place. She found herself resting in God. She felt utterly set free. "i just want to hang out with God! i can't keep the smile off my face!" she wrote.

After that, her emails went back and forth between the peace and joy she felt in her relationship with God and her anxiety about what was going to happen in her life as a result. She began to sense strongly that she should leave the Mormon Church. I found myself so freed of myself, so fully on board with whatever God was doing with Mollie, that I argued for slowing down and not leaving so quickly. I reminded her of her own words, that all that mattered to her was God, and suggested that if moving so fast to do what she thought God had told her to do was making her lose sight of God, she could stop and reset and trust God to keep leading her.

Mollie's aim was no longer about finding the right answers, or the right framework. It was no longer about going after God, or trying to find God, as though pursuing an idea or achieving a goal. Now her life was about the relationship, the dialogue, the interaction with the Divine. Hers was a quest of belonging in relationship with the living God.

> i've never in my life felt so connected to God!
>
> it's exciting and overwhelming at the same time. it scares me because i feel so open and vulnerable. i know i shouldn't feel scared, but i have always felt that when you really open yourself up, you're opening yourself up to hurt. so i guess it's hard for me to be so connected.

Mollie ended up being accepted to the same discipleship training program I had done, on the Mercy Ship. Her faith continued to deepen; her joy continued to expand. "i feel like i am learning so much every day about who God is and what it is like to live knowing Him." Even as she navigated painfully letting yet another deeply invested life go—releasing all the structures and relationships she'd committed to so fully and stepping into the unknown—she did so with a sense of trust and courage that inspired and instructed me.

A few weeks later I heard back from Fuller Seminary. I was accepted into the MDiv program. But there was another envelope in the mail from Fuller alongside the thick acceptance packet. It was a single sheet, a half-page rejection letter. The spiritual direction concentration was for people age thirty and older, it said. I was twenty-one. "Thank you for applying, but you do not meet the minimum age requirement for this program. When you arrive on campus, though, feel free to stop in and have a conversation with the director if you'd like to know more."

Surprise and disappointment flooded me. It had seemed so clear. All of what I had been through with Mollie seemed to be leading me right to this thing. What was God up to? But I was also buoyed by the incredible thing I was witnessing with Mollie. God was trustworthy. I believed God would lead me. If this was not what I was meant to be doing, something else would become clear. I decided to continue pursuing a master of divinity degree without the spiritual direction concentration.

A few months later I arrived on the sunlit, palm-tree-lined streets of Southern California with my college roommate, in my tightly packed 1993 Dodge Colt hatchback. We pulled up and excitedly unloaded our belongings into the souped-up, two-room shed we were renting behind someone's Pasadena home. Two hours later I walked my twenty-one-year-old midwestern grunge self—dressed in baggy men's shorts;

a thrift-store, button-down plaid shirt; and green Converse All Star high-top sneakers, with my unshaven legs and Alanis Morissette hair down to my waist—into the office of the director of the spiritual direction concentration.

I had no expectations other than to introduce myself and have a conversation, as the letter had invited. We ended up talking for an hour about many things, including Mollie. She told me I was an old soul in a young body. When she said that, I felt seen.

At the end of the conversation, to my surprise, Dr. Libbie Patterson leaned back and threw her thin, expressive hands up in the air and laughed. She leaned toward me with her elbows on her knees and said, "Kara, I can't believe I am going to say this, but I believe you belong in this program." She told me to talk to a pastor I trusted and a psychology professor of mine from college who had begun studying in a spiritual direction program. "Spend some time in prayer and discernment, and get back to me."

That fall I started learning spiritual direction. I was introduced to the mystics and spent my days reading Saint John of the Cross, Saint Ignatius of Loyola, Saint Teresa of Avila, and Evelyn Underhill. I entered into spiritual direction myself, with someone accompanying me in my deepening relationship with God, helping me sense God's movements and invitations. And alongside Greek, Hebrew, and biblical interpretation, I began studying discernment, spiritual disciplines, and prayer.

Spiritual direction grounds everything in the trust that God is already here, already doing something, and it is our job to pay attention and join in. This resonated in my bones, fed me to my core, and began laying the foundation in me for all that was to come.

We have a word in our house that means something real but for which there is no English word. When Maisy was just a few weeks old, we left her one afternoon napping on our bed alone. We all went downstairs and neglected to turn on the baby monitor. By the time we realized she was crying an hour later, she had sent herself into a frenzy, red-faced and furious, kicking and waving her arms and wailing at the top of her lungs.

When we finally heard her and realized what the sound was, we took the stairs two at a time, flew to her side, and piled on the bed, crooning and comforting and reaching for her, "It's OK! Maisy! We're here, sweetie. We're so sorry! You're OK now!" Not quite three-year-old Owen laid his hands on her chest and leaned his head down on the bed near her cheek and said tenderly and wisely, "Oh Maisy, don't worry, honey. It was only hoatis. It's OK, baby. You just had hoatis."

Andy and I shrugged at each other in confusion, and then Andy cleared his throat and asked, "Owen, what's *hoatis*?"

Owen glanced up from comforting his sister and said to us, matter-of-factly, "You know. *Hoatis*. When you're all alone and crying and nobody hears you."[1]

Hoatis. It's a real thing. There needed to be a word for that.

Here are some other words that describe real things, for which there is no English equivalent:

Tartle. Scottish: "The act of hesitating while introducing someone because you've forgotten their name."

Jayus. Indonesian: "A joke so poorly told and so unfunny that one cannot help but laugh."

Torschlusspanik. German: Translated literally, this word means "gate-closing panic," but in usage, it refers to "the fear of diminishing opportunities as one ages."

Tingo. Pascuense (Easter Island): "The act of taking objects one desires from the house of a friend by gradually borrowing all of them."[2]

Life is full of things and experiences that we don't quite have the words to describe. One of these realities is addressed 2,617 times in the Old Testament with a Hebrew word for which we have no English equivalent. That word is *hesed*. It's *hesed* that the Psalmist raves about in song, *hesed* that sustains the patriarchs and matriarchs in all their blundering and barrenness, *hesed* that saves children of Israel out of Egypt, and *hesed* that gives them the words of life in the wilderness. *Hesed* is the gift meant to be reveled in at Sabbath, studied in Scripture, sung of in worship, and practiced in daily life. One might even say *hesed* describes the true substance of this whole story of God, of which our own lives are a tiny but significant piece. *Hesed* is hidden within the ordinary fabric of life, all life, *our lives*. It powerfully binds, upholds, and communicates *what all of life is about.*

So what does *hesed* mean? It has sometimes been translated as "mercy," and certainly that's a part—that undeserved forgiveness, compassion, and grace—but mercy doesn't nearly capture it. *Hesed* is more mutual, more communal than mercy. Another way it's been translated is "loving-kindness." And yes, it feels like kindness, and undoubtedly it is full of love. But kindness can be impersonal, and love—at least in English—sounds too much like a feeling. *Hesed* is more intimate than kindness and more bonding than love, or rather, *it calls love to be more bonding.* It has also been translated as loyalty. And this gets even closer, because it *is* a "through thick and thin," "no matter what" kind of faithfulness and constancy. But loyalty can be exclusive, and *hesed* is broad and inclusive. It spreads wider as it reaches out, bringing in others, and still others.

One might even try calling it "friendship," in the classic sense, not the Facebook sense. Friendship as chosen love and commitment, not demanded by bloodlines or desired for personal gain, not for networking or nostalgia. Generous, really seeing an other and desiring their best, choosing to be with and for them, sacrificing oneself even, for their well-being. *Hesed* is like friendship but deeper, thicker, richer; it is what gives friendship its strength.

Perhaps the best way to think about *hesed* is something like "belongingness." It is the inner logic of belonging, the substance of it. It looks like compassion, mercy and loyalty, loving-kindness and friendship. It looks like choosing over and over again to be there with and for this other, no matter what and without end. *"The steadfast love [hesed] of the Lord never ceases, his mercies [hesed] never comes to an end"* (Lamentations 3:22).

Hesed says, *I will go there with you. Hesed* forgives. It hopes. It prays. It sits at his bedside every day, even when the memory has faded and he no longer knows you are there. It stands by you when everybody else has fallen away; even if you deserved for them to, it won't desert you. It drives across the country to settle you into your first house or moves her into your house when she's too sick to care for herself. When you hold that new life in your arms for the first time, *Hesed* is that sudden, jolting realization that you will forever and always now belong to this one. You are now part of belongingness with them. To belong greatly extends our being; it stretches and lengthens us beyond our selves, beyond the moment. You will Be. Long. Like *forever* long. *Long* will you *be* for these others.[3] And that's just the fleeting and frail human participation in *hesed!* That's just the tiny tastes we share of belongingness here and now. It's far bigger than all of that. Bigger, even, than we could ever begin to conceive of in our wildest imagination.

Hesed is the voice God spoke into nothing and made life. *Hesed* is the breath of God that animated human spirit and formed in God's own image—like the belongingness within God's own self Father, Son, and Spirit—a new creature of belonging, a new community of life to whom to belong. *You belong to me; I belong to you. My precious creation, my life, my love. And I will stop at nothing to cherish you in this belonging; I will never leave you or forsake you. I am the Lord your God.*

One whole book of the Bible is a story of *hesed*, of belongingness. Ruth is the story of a Moabite woman married to the son of a Judean couple living in Moab. When their son dies, Ruth leaves her people to move to Judah with her widowed mother-in-law. It is belongingness that drives Ruth to stand with Naomi, who by law has nobody left to care for her, and God's belongingness moves the whole story. Ruth should have stayed with her people and remarried, started her life over at home. That was the wise thing, the right thing to do. But instead, she took the way of *hesed*. She stayed with Naomi.

What could Ruth do for Naomi, really? She had nothing to give—she was not a man, so she had no standing or property or means of supporting her. She could do absolutely nothing for Naomi but be with her, share her position, her journey, her currently miserable lot in life. She could give Naomi belongingness; she could share her *hesed*. "Where you go, I will go; . . . your people shall be my people, and your God my God. Where you die, I will die—there will I be buried" (Ruth 1:16–17). *I will give up my own security and future to accompany you, come what may.*

So the story of this woman—this widow, this foreigner with nothing to give and no future in front of her—became the story of the people of Israel, the story of King David, the story of Jesus Christ. Ruth had *no idea* she was doing anything more than joining her own seemingly insignificant life to the seemingly insignificant life of her friend. She certainly didn't intend to become—for the people of this God she didn't even know yet—the bearer of *hesed*, the bringer of belonging.

Nestled within the Old Testament collection of laws and leaders, priests and posturing, battles and conquering, defeat and redemption, is this intimate little story, tucked in there amid all that testosterone. In this humble tale, we don't hear the voice of God or see the hand of God smiting or waving or cheering or punishing. We don't witness big sweeping judgments or wide arcing redemption. We just observe these few ordinary people living their ordinary lives, trying to survive the best they can, broken and without hope, but moving forward anyway the best way they know how. In and through them, we witness the heart of God.

And in the divine sense of humor, or direction, or both, God chose *this* story to remind God's people who they were and whose they were. As the Old Testament unfolds, we learn that future generations forgot who they were, what they were meant to be about, and they sought to remove foreigners from their midst to maintain their pure identity. For them, God uses *this* story as a reminder that what made them the people of God was not their bloodline, their security, their wealth, or their knowledge. It wasn't their leadership or good manners or connections or power, and it wasn't their piety. They did not earn or deserve their identity as the people of this God. What made them God's people was nothing less than the incomprehensible belongingness of God. It was God's *hesed* that defined them. God is a relentless belongingness kind of God, and they were to be God's radical belongingness kind of people. God says, *You are my people and I am your God. I am God because of you. And I am God in spite of you. You are mine, and I am yours. And my belongingness moves within and between you, but also beyond and outside of you. And just in case you forget, or maybe because you will quite often forget, it is really important that the person who carries forward your story, my story, is none other than Ruth, the widowed Moabite foreigner.*

At the end of the story, when Boaz, the kinsmen of Naomi's husband, decides to take Ruth as his wife, the towns-people and elders say to him, "We are witnesses. May the

Lord make the woman who is coming into your house like Rachel and Leah, who together built up the house of Israel" (Ruth 4:11).

> So Boaz took Ruth and she became his wife. When they came together, the Lord made her conceive, and she bore a son. Then the women said to Naomi, "Blessed be the Lord, who has not left you this day without next-of-kin; and may his name be renowned in Israel! He shall be to you a restorer of life and a nourisher of your old age; for your daughter-in-law who loves you, who is more to you than seven sons, has borne him. . . ." They named him Obed; he became the father of Jesse, the father of David. (Ruth 4:13–17)

From outside the human places of power and possibility— by the barrenness of widows, the weakness of women, and the otherness of foreigners—God moves in *hesed* once again to bring life and hope to a people. "I will go there with you," they said. "You will not be alone."

In our poverty or abundance, strength or weakness, joy or sorrow, fullness or barrenness, pain or delight, right there, every day, *we belong*. And right there, every day, we are invited to *Be. Long.* with each other. God claims us in a wide embrace of unending belongingness and stirs us to join in extending that embrace. In a world of *hoatis*, the deepest reality is *hesed*: we belong to God, and we belong to each other.

We had been praying for Marty as a congregation ever since his diagnosis, but now things shifted. One obvious change was that Marty now knew that he was going to die sooner rather than later. But the real shift was that he was willing to share the whole process with us and let us in on it. He wasn't going to keep his pain or suffering a secret. He was willing to let us minister to him, but honestly, courageously, *as a minister himself*. He was willing to witness to the rest of us to the reality of dying that every one of us will face at some point. He was going to be a leader in his vulnerability. He was going to help us all live into belongingness.

Two weeks later, on Palm Sunday, I stood before the congregation, near the communion table that just a few months earlier had held Marty's birthday cupcake. I ended my sermon by announcing to the church that Marty was dying.

"In a few minutes," I said, "we will gather around Marty and give thanks to God for God's calling on Marty's life. And because death is coming for every one of us at some point, we will say out loud that Marty is dying, and you guys, I feel really sad about that." I felt the tears well up, and I paused for a minute, gulped them down, and repeated, "I feel so sad." After a moment, I continued, letting my firm conviction fill my voice:

But we will also say that God is still God, and God is with us, and God is with Marty. And in these coming weeks, we will be saying, as the crowds did, along the roadway on Palm Sunday, *Save us!* And just as they did when they waved their palm branches thinking Jesus was a conquering king, we will mean all sorts of different things by it, and God will hear it anyway, and

God will save us, because this is what God does and who God is.

There is more beauty and hope and love and joy that God wants to impart into Marty's life, and into all of our lives, as we share them with each other, so we will not be afraid. And even when we are, a little, still, we will walk with Marty. Because this is where Jesus is.

Jesus walks this way with us. Jesus went this way before us in this prophetic parade. This confusing, strange spectacle, where truth was spoken right into illusion, right through delusions, and when they called him *king* and praised him for it, what was happening was bigger and truer than any of them could have realized at the time. And so we trust that by facing death instead of fearing it, we are also part of something that is bigger and truer than we can realize.

"We are all dying," I told my stricken people, "but Marty is out ahead of us on the journey that each of us will one day walk. And so Marty is uniquely called to minister to the rest of us through this experience."

There is a power to ritual. We are creatures of symbolism and meaning-seeking. We are capable of experiencing far more than we can see and hear and touch and say, but we need these things we can see and hear and touch and say in order to enter into the deeper meaning of experiences. In rituals, we allow ordinary things to become a gateway to transcendent reality. Water, bread, wine—these things are just these things, but they are also so much more. They are vehicles of story, carriers of meaning, catalysts of connection—*elements*, we call them. Oil is one of these elements.

Throughout our faith history and the biblical narrative, anointing someone with oil has been a way of blessing, of marking a significant milestone, or of offering spiritual protection. We put it on the head of the sick in prayers for healing or as a seal over them on their deathbed. We anoint those who are departing for a long journey. When someone is baptized, we make the sign of the cross on their foreheads in oil, sealing them in a covenant with God and inaugurating their life journey as one who has died already and been raised into newness of life with Christ.[4] And in Scripture, when people are set aside for a role to which they are called by God, such as a prophet or a king, they are anointed as a way for us to acknowledge and for them to receive that calling. Jesus himself recognized his own calling: "The Spirit of the Lord is upon me, because he has anointed me to bring good news to the poor. He has sent me to proclaim release to the captives and recovery of sight to the blind, to let the oppressed go free" (Luke 4:18).

Our human performance of this ritual creates a moment in which we are open to transcendence. It is a moment in mystery when God, who is always near, comes near. Rituals signify something God actually does. In this ceremony we were about to do with Marty, we were affirming God's blessing and calling of Marty, and he was receiving this call and accepting a unique and distinctive role among us. As in all holy moments, our deepest belonging was made manifest here: we felt our belonging to God, who was calling Marty to minister among us, and we felt our belonging to each other as the community that was affirming God's call on Marty. And Marty was receiving his blessed new role.

I called Marty forward. He edged his way past the legs and canes of the women sharing his pew. They laid their hands on his arm as he passed, like a gentle current carrying him to shore. When he reached the front, I placed my hand on his shoulder and addressed the congregation:

> Today we are commissioning Marty to a Ministry of Dying. What this means is that Marty is saying yes to a form of leadership by example, a willingness to share his journey with us and let us share this experience with him. Marty is not called to put on a good attitude or wow us with his witty wisdom and end of life insight. He is simply called to be honest and true, not to hide his pain or questions, but to allow us to share in them with him.
>
> Where Marty goes, we will go, and we will be his people (Ruth 1:16), alongside him in this journey as far as we can accompany him, until he takes the final steps with Christ alone, into the everlasting arms of God's love.

And then I turned to Marty, while the congregation looked on, some of them openly weeping. "Marty, God has called you to particular service, and the Holy Spirit will give you all you need to fulfill this calling. Do you welcome the responsibility of this calling among us, to a Ministry of Dying?"

Marty looked back at me. He was the only steady person in the room. With calm confidence, he answered, "I do."

Then I turned to the congregation. Their courage and tenderness radiated toward Marty and me. Gratitude filled me, and I felt a stab of love for them all. I cleared my throat and asked them, "Do you confirm the call of God on our brother Marty to live his journey of life and death alongside us as a blessing and witness of God's grace?"

"We do," they echoed back.

"Will you support and encourage him in this ministry?" I asked.

"We will," they answered.

I opened a small gold container, a "stock," containing a cotton ball soaked in oil. I blotted my thumb on it and raised it to Marty's forehead. Pressing it onto his skin, I made a cross and said, "Marty, child of the covenant, I sign you with the cross that you may remember that in life and in death, you belong to God, and be thankful."

I invited the congregation to come forward, and they streamed out of their pews and gathered around Marty to pray for him. Warm bodies crowded around me, breath and touch enveloped us. The children wiggled their way into the center so that Marty was surrounded first by a circle of small people, each reaching up and resting their fingers on his back or stomach like a belt of tiny hands. Then a ring of adults encircled the children, hands resting on Marty's shoulders and head, and people beyond them reached out to touch those who were touching him. Marty was cocooned inside stretching arms and transparent faces beaming love at him, a physical expression of God's love holding him. And we prayed for our friend.

When we finished, we lifted our heads, dropped our arms, and smiled at Marty. He smiled back. I looked into his face, with his congregation gathered around us, and announced, "Marty, you are hereby commissioned to a Ministry of Dying. May the God of peace guide you in every way and keep your whole being—spirit, soul, and body—in God's loving care, until the day you are united body and spirit completely with God—Father, Son, and Holy Spirit—for all eternity. Amen."

We tend to think certain things—sickness, sin, sorrow, dying, or distress, for example—disqualify us from living, or loving, or *being*. We think we need to avoid or overcome those things in order to live. We try to be stronger, more faithful, more put-together, less human, so that we can somehow reach God, or meaning, or whatever feels most like actually living. But Jesus, who became human, is encountered not by avoiding the weakness of our humanity, but by embracing it.

Because of Jesus, the place where God meets us, really and truly and actually, isn't in fact with the confident and strong. Jesus is always hanging out with the weak and the honest, the ones who can't fake it, the dying, and the ones who are brave enough to admit it. All experiences of authentic humanity—weakness, courage, ministry, and living—begin in honesty. The Holy One is encountered, not hypothetically or figuratively, not in power and might, but *actually encountered* in vulnerability and weakness. God is *always* breaking in, in ways we don't often expect or respect.

In Jesus Christ, the trajectory of all things is forever bent back toward God. All things are moving toward their completion, redemption, and wholeness. And you and I are held within this movement so that even in the darkest times, when death is breathing down our necks, something greater even than death is holding us fast, never letting us go.

The opposite of rejection and barrenness and impossibility, nothingness, is *being*. God breathes existence into being *ex nihilo*, out of nothing. God brings hope and salvation through the barrenness and impossibility of all those matriarchs and patriarchs of our Scriptures. God comes into our own nothingness and brings forth life. We are called out of nonbeing, every day, by the great *I am* to *be*. Be who we are. Be where we are. Be with God right here, where God already and always is, waiting for us.

Jesus already embodies this way of living. He is always living his true being—fully God, fully human, fully right here and now. He opens this way of life to us. The doorway to transcendence is *right here*. In our own raw and unpolished lives, God is with us, bearing our pain and sharing our joy. And we can actually *see* God-with-us when we are with and for each other, bearing each other's pain and sharing each other's joy.

The day we commissioned Marty to a Ministry of Dying was a holy moment we stepped into together. We were fully human, fully present, with each other and with God. Telling the truth of our vulnerability and our hope, our need and our courage, submitting to the call of God and welcoming the presence of God in our midst—in that moment we were the church being church. Any religious structure, institution, or system is just the container that either restricts or creates space for us to experience our belonging to God and each other. I'd begun learning this alongside Mollie. I was rediscovering it again as I watched that space open up in the congregation's commitment to share Marty's journey with him and his commitment to share his reality with them. This formal role he had accepted, this structure we'd just established, held us together and opened us wider to God and each other. We can always choose to share life with each other. God is already here, already doing something; it is our job to pay attention and join in. By acknowledging Marty's singular leadership and ministry among us, we were paying attention. We were joining in. That's church.

Immediately after worship, Marty was joined at coffee hour by three other men who, while loquacious in matters of geopolitics, the history of world wars, or obscure first-century religious sects, usually clammed up when talk turned personal. But this time their conversation was different. One asked Marty how he was feeling, nodding as Marty described his symptoms and tentatively wondering aloud what the next stages might be like for him. Another offered to drive Marty any time he might need a ride to an appointment, and the others seconded his offer. And then one man shared about his prostate cancer, something he had revealed to only a few others before then. Leaning in, they all listened and offered encouragement and support to him, to Marty, to one another.

I watched this unfold and felt my breath catch. I raised my eyes to meet those of an elder standing on the opposite side of the room. Sue had also noticed this small gathering. She placed her hand on her heart and looked back at me, slowly shaking her head in wonder.

Marty's ministry had begun.

Chapter 4

In Godforsakenness

Lazarus Blessing

The secret
of this blessing
is that it is written
on the back
of what binds you.

To read
this blessing,
you must take hold
of the end
of what
confines you,
must begin to tug
at the edge
of what wraps
you round.

It may take long
and long
for its length
to fall away,
for the words
of this blessing
to unwind
in folds
about your feet.

By then
you will no longer
need them.

By then this blessing
will have pressed itself
into your waking flesh,
will have passed
into your bones,
will have traveled
every vein

until it comes to rest
inside the chambers
of your heart
that beats to
the rhythm
of benediction

and the cadence
of release.

        —JAN RICHARDSON, *Circle of Grace*

With all humility I say, it is God who should ask for forgiveness, not we, Him. Someday you will know this. A saint could explain.

—SAINT TERESA OF AVILA,
The Way of Perfection

*A*fter we commissioned Marty to a Ministry of Dying, something again shifted in the congregation. There was room for—indeed, the expectation of—honesty, forthrightness about his journey. We were expected to ask. He was expected to answer. He was dying. We all knew it. For someone to be living so openly and vulnerably among us felt strange and holy and simultaneously quite natural and ordinary. We found strength in standing together in our weakness, our helplessness to stop what was happening, and our commitment not to back down from the discomfort but to remain there together. And as Marty was painfully letting his deeply invested life go, gradually releasing all the structures and relationships he had committed to so fully and stepping into the unknown, he did so with a sense of trust and courage that inspired and instructed us all.

Throughout my college years, a vague depression had been building in my family—a distance and despair hanging over our house like a cloud. I was living on my college campus forty minutes away. I popped back home from time to time on the weekends but missed the full impact of it. I could tell, though, that my three younger sisters weren't doing great. I'd heard about big parties they'd thrown when my parents were gone; they were skipping school, trying drugs. They all smoked but didn't want to lead each other astray, so they never smoked in front of each other. Instead, they'd take turns standing over the knothole on our side deck, a tiny opening to an ever-mounting heap of cigarette and joint butts piling up beneath the house. My mom was palpably sad. She regularly shouted bitter accusations at my dad. Her anger and grief tainted every interaction. So he avoided her, which made her more angry and sad.

My dad was traveling a lot. When he was home, he hid behind his closed office door. Previously the very model of an engaged father, he now felt to us to be utterly inaccessible. One afternoon, I called him and asked him to meet me for lunch. He loved us. His family was the important thing in his life. *He must not realize how bad it is*, I thought. *He must not know how he is affecting us.* I was sure this lunch with his eldest daughter and some truth spoken in love would shake him out of whatever this was and bring him back to us. Over burgers at a wall-cluttered neighborhood chain restaurant, I told him I was really worried about whatever was going on with him. "The family is learning to function without you," I pleaded. "Come back." He just looked at me sadly and said nothing at all. I returned to my college dorm room alarmed and confused.

At the same time that things were breaking open in a good way for my friend Mollie, they were breaking open in a peculiar and terrible way for my family. My two youngest sisters dropped out of high school and ostensibly "home-schooled," but I'm not entirely clear what they actually did with their time. My parents' supervision waned dramatically, and they both seemed to find more and more support—or distraction—away from home. My youngest sister hung out a lot with my college friends and me. My dad was so absent that his eyes had gone dull; when I looked at him, I couldn't see *him* anymore.

When I arrived in Southern California to begin seminary, I was ready for adventure and eager to head into the great whatever-was-next. The tension back home that I was fleeing couldn't follow me here. The worry and anxiety that were building about my family took a back seat to my new life about to begin. I jumped in with both feet.

I became an ecclesiastical tourist. My religious curiosity awakened, I visited every kind of church I could find. Each one opened something in me a little wider, softened something, made me more alert somehow to the presence and grace of God.

I shared the previously unheard-of (to me) Ash Wednesday with the Catholics. There I started weeping when a very old, bent-over woman in front of me received the ashes on her forehead as the priest intoned, "From dust you came and to dust you shall return," and I didn't stop crying until I was back in the pew with my own forehead smeared in the mark of death.

On Easter Sunday I joined the Episcopalians, rising before the sun and making my way into an ornately carved pew in a sanctuary filled with lilies. There, trumpets and a procession of clergy in vestments welcomed me into Easter with a fanfare like none I had ever known. I loved the Brethren for their coffee-hour letter writing to politicians and the Nazarenes for their faithful, frankly spoken prayers. I discovered Lent with the Methodists, sitting with goose bumps through my first Tenebrae service as the candles were extinguished one by one until we were plunged into the darkness of Good Friday. I celebrated Advent with the laid-back UCC folks and their beautiful poetry and 1970s folk songs. The singing at the Congregational Church was my favorite, and the Presbyterians *brought* the sermons.

For the first time in my whole life, I heard the Apostles' Creed. I read written liturgy aloud with others; I was bathed in incense. For the first time, I knelt in church—pulling down the little bench from the pew in front of me made for just that purpose. For the first time, I made the sign of the cross over myself, which I had only ever seen done in the movies. And for the first time, I watched people recite *from memory*, in unison, words that had been said by the faithful for centuries, their voices rising and falling in waves.

I was shocked to discover that "worship" didn't refer to just the forty minutes of song time; for most churches, it meant the *whole service*, sometimes with little or no singing. I was likewise stunned to discover that sermons were very rarely the forty-five-minute-long biblical expositions I had grown up with. And they generally didn't go chronologically through a book of the Bible, one verse at a time (like our pastor had, who'd spent seven years getting through Matthew). In fact, in some traditions, they often hopped *all around the Bible.* And some sermons were as short as two minutes, in which case, I learned, they are called "homilies."

What I had known to be church had felt so sure and final, so expansive, so all-in-all. But it turned out that there was so much more. Our great big important megachurch was merely one tiny expression, one single note in the vast harmony, *one skin cell* in the body of Christ.

Church, it turned out, was so much greater than myself and my world; it was eternal. It stretches out before us and beyond us and reaches around the whole planet. There are many different ways to gather for worship. There are many different ways to be a congregation. There are many different ways to be a Christian. The practices of church come to life in a breathless array of traditions and interpretations, languages, emphases, and forms that have been adapted over time, expanded and contracted, that are molded by culture and that form culture. Churches are big and small, weak and strong, sick and healthy, old and young, boring and dry as a mouthful of sawdust, and so heart-achingly beautiful they made my legs weak. There is no end to the variety in human beings' ways of relating to and experiencing our relationship with God. The gift it is to be in this thing called church began to dawn on me. I felt awe at encountering this mysterious, messy, broad, and colorful reality with endless expressions and extraordinary possibilities.

Also, in my new California life, I met Andy. We'd come from the same Christian liberal arts college in Minnesota but there had been no reason for our paths to cross. He was the hockey goalie and darling of the campus ministry office; I hung out in coffee shops and the back woods with the alternative kids. But in SoCal, the Minnesota contingent was small and tight. The five of us (my college roommate and I, Andy, and two others) hung out on occasional Sunday mornings at a local sports dive to eat nachos and watch the ten o'clock Vikings' football games. To accommodate for his dyslexia, Andy had hired my roommate to proofread his papers. One day she was sick, and I filled in. Aside from the funny, engaging Andy I had begun to know, I suddenly also saw the depth of his creativity and intelligence as I teased out his original and profound ideas from under misspelled words and convoluted grammar. Turns out I was a more interested and engaged proofreader than my roommate had been, so I kept the job after that, and we began hanging out together more and more. We were so different from one another and so different from one another's ideal partner; it was obvious to us both that there was no risk of this becoming anything other than a great friendship.

My first winter in Southern California I went home for a strange and strained Christmas break. On Christmas morning, with Bing Crosby crooning in the background, our family gathered next to the tree we could only muster the energy to put lights on, having left all the precious family ornaments packed away for the first time in family history. We opened gifts, while my dad sat on the couch in a red plaid nightshirt and sweatpants with an incongruous Santa hat drooping off his head, biting his lip while tears rolled steadily and inexplicably down his cheeks.

My favorite gift that year was a Dictaphone (a handheld cassette-tape machine for recording class lectures). When we sat down at the table for Christmas dinner, I slipped it out of my pocket onto my lap and hit *record*. I was going to test out this bad boy. A few minutes into the perfectly normal holiday meal, my sister Erin, who loves to mark significant moments with meaningful conversation, asked, "Where does everyone want to be this time next year?"

We went around the table, adding our random thoughts. I actually can't remember anything anyone else said, though, because when we got to my mom, she answered, "This time next year I want to be in a happy marriage or in heaven."

I softly clicked off the Dictaphone in my lap and stopped breathing. Nobody moved. Forks were held suspended in the air, our eyes wide. Then I gently pressed my finger back down on the Dictaphone record button. For the next hour, my family spilled out drama and sorrow, confusion and frustration, arguing and yelling without offering or hearing a lot of answers. At one point, Erin, voice high with strain and tears, looked across the table at my dad and pleaded, "Dad! What big secret is so important that you're willing to lose your family over it?" There was no answer.

It was a brutal and horrifying Christmas dinner. *And I have it all on tape.*

After that, things staggered on at home, getting steadily bleaker. My family was unraveling. Erin left home right after high school graduation, at seventeen, to attend a nine-month, charismatic, dispensational, fundamentalist Christian discipleship program in Middle America. Jesi followed her as soon as she turned eighteen. Callie, fourteen, was left at home alone with our increasingly erratic parents. Even though I was kept abreast of the developments and heard painful reports from my sisters, I was largely emotionally oblivious to how bad things were getting with my family. My days were spent in class or at coffee shops with theology and history books open in front of me, or behind the front desk of the student finance office. Evenings and weekends Andy and I meandered the streets of Old Town Pasadena, met at the movies, lingered in our favorite juice bar, and dipped our toes into the Southern California music scene where our friend Elliot frequently played with his band. There was nobody either of us would rather have spent time with, and being together started to feel more normal than being apart. Our "safe" friendship was developing into an unexpected and unlikely romance that took us a long time to acknowledge.

One evening, in the middle of my second year in seminary, about a month after Andy and I finally acknowledged we were in it for the long haul and became engaged, I got a phone call from my dad. I was standing in the living room of my second-floor apartment. The sun was setting, and the sky was pink over the San Rafael Hills. I asked my dad to hold on while I closed the windows against the relentless roar of the traffic on the 210 freeway, over which my apartment was perched.

"Hey, Dad!" I said. "What's up?"

His voice was flat and weary. He cleared his throat. "Well, your mom took my computer to an IT expert, and she found some disturbing things on it."

"What things, Dad? What are you talking about?" I felt the blood drain from my head, and my hands started tingling. I thought I might pass out. I couldn't make sense of what I was hearing. What was this conversation?

"It doesn't matter," he answered. "It's there. She's asked me to move out. I'm moving out."

"What are you talking about? What's going on?" I yelled. I was crying. I wiped the snot off my face with my sleeve. He just kept apologizing. Then he hung up.

I was shaking. I didn't know what to do with myself. Whatever had been building, the secret he'd been keeping, it had detonated. And my world was rocked. Nothing made sense.

I tried calling Andy, but he wasn't home. I ran to my room and grabbed my keys and purse and took the stairs two at a time down to my car. I drove a few blocks to the supermarket, slammed the car into park, and shut off the ignition. I plunged through the doors into the florescent-lit store and made a beeline for the bakery. *What had the most chocolate?* I grabbed a heart-shaped, chocolate-frosted cake off a gaudy, pink and red Valentine's Day display table and bought it.

When I got back to my apartment, I threw the cake on the table. I felt hysterical, unhinged. Filled with adrenaline and rage, I stormed down the hallway and pounded on my roommate's door.

"Come in!" she called. She and her boyfriend were lounging on the bed, books around them and a laptop open on her lap.

"My fucking parents are apparently splitting up!" I screeched. They froze, eyes wide, taking me in. I was heaving and frantic. Then I burst into wild laughter. "I just bought a fucking chocolate cake!" I shouted. "Come eat it with me!"

So they came. And that's what we did.

Just seven months before my own wedding, my parents' marriage ended, and our family ended with it. My parents divorced and moved into separate apartments; their turn inward to self-preservation was complete. When the dust cleared, my sisters and I found ourselves strewn about the rubble of our family trying to figure out how to stand and stutter out of childhood into adulthood on our own.

My youngest sister, Callie, got her GED at sixteen, worked as a waitress, and slept on the couches of friends and strangers. There were huge surprise debts that needed covering, so the family cabin was sold. Then the house and the five acres it sat on were sold. It took only weeks for a developer to chop our land into quarter-acre lots and sell it to other developers, who began building new suburban homes all over what had once been quiet fields and woodlands. Our own house and yard were sold to the city of Maple Grove, which handed it over to the fire department. Our family home was subsequently burned to the ground in a firefighter training exercise.

The annihilation was sweeping and complete. There was nothing left of my invincible, exceptional family and nowhere for any of us to go home to. We were six individuals, scattered around the country, fending for ourselves.

Across the street from where our house stood was a white clapboard one-room schoolhouse and an old, tiny, tidy Irish cemetery. In the center of the cemetery stands the only tree, huge and breathtaking. At the base of the tree is the grave of a baby, Annie Donahue, buried there more than 120 years ago. The sapling planted at her grave now shades over half the cemetery. During my adolescent years, I used to jog along the small path around the graves and sit with my journal under that tree.

I was not there when my family house was destroyed; I lived far away from the epicenter of my family's ruin. But several years later I would work up the courage to go back and see the place where our home had been. I would walk around in shock at the razed site and unrecognizable topography. Then I would head for the familiar comfort of the cemetery and end up back under that tree.

That day, years later, I would write this in my journal:

I am sitting under Annie Donahue's tree looking across the street at the mound that was my home. There's some sort of structure there, a utility building built into the side of a huge dirt hill. It's as though instead of knocking down our house they just buried it, and if I just brushed the dirt off the top of the middle of that hill, I'd find our chimney or maybe uncover the skylight to my bedroom and be able to look in and see my forest green carpeting below.

It was strange being over there. I couldn't really make out just where things used to be, exactly. There are no trees, no brush, no natural distinguishing marks of any kind—even the shape of the earth is different. From over here I can see in my mind's eye where the house stood, and the glorious tree in the yard, the huge split pine with the treehouse nestled in the branches, and the row of rose bushes along the western edge of the yard. Now it is all mud and dirt, an oblong hill with a brick building slapped on the front of it.

I felt like if I only walked around, I may uncover something we left outside, a board from the treehouse, even one tiger lily from the roadside, but it's like I was standing there making it all up, like we had never really been there at all.

I wonder what happened to the yard swing?

The only thing left at all is the very beginning of our driveway. It's exactly the same shape, with exactly the same gravel—but after 5 feet it stops, and the foreign, muddy hill surrounded by the sounds of progress and development begins.

So I am sitting under Annie Donahue's tree. And I am grieving for my dead and buried.

The mailbox is still there. My grave marker. My reminder. Only survived because it's on this side of the street—like that weakest and most trivial of links was spared, standing as if nothing has changed. There is even a recent newspaper in the paper box. Like someone didn't tell them it's gone. I feel like sending my past a letter, commemorating the family who died and was buried there with the mailbox still standing. I want to tell its story—my family, my home.

I guess I am not rootless, disconnected, when I come here. I guess I have somewhere to come home to. I come home here to remember the life and death of us, our childhood. Our family breathed its last in this place.

I want someone to come by and ask me, "Which grave are you visiting?" So that I can point to the fresh black mound and tell them, "My family lived there; there is where my home is buried."

When my family fell apart, the iron scaffolding of my inner world collapsed. I was plunged into a darkness with no light, a well of grief with no bottom. This sounds like hyperbole, but it is how I felt. All my bearings were gone; my compass was broken. My ability to tell what was real or good or trustworthy in the world was lost.

Unable to sort truth from lies, and so distrustful of my own radar, I stopped speaking to my dad for several months. I cried at inopportune times and unpredictable moments. Food lost taste, colors dimmed. (I didn't even know this had happened until a year later when, quite suddenly, while I was jogging around the Rose Bowl, in fits and flashes, shocking green returned to the leaves and brilliant blue to the sky above me. It stopped me in my tracks and took my breath away.)

Life had lost all guarantees, except the guarantee, it seemed, of suffering, of death. I only wanted to stay home, but even that didn't feel safe. God was entirely absent. I felt afraid of everything—plane rides, earthquakes—because I felt like now *anything* could happen.

Night after night I ended up at Andy's apartment, sleeping on his couch because I couldn't bear to be alone. In the morning I would shuffle home in my pajamas and slippers with my pillow under my arm, conscious of the married seminary couples peeking out their windows at me and getting absolutely the wrong idea about what went on these nights. (They probably didn't picture so much fully clothed crying.) I was still doing my life—I trudged around the school campus, I sat in my classes, I ate and slept—but all the while I felt like a dead person. A person who was dead inside.

The day my invincible faith finally died began with a phone call. My sister Erin called me from the end-timesy Christian community in Missouri, where she and my sister Jesi had been living and working without pay, and excitedly shared that her Bible study the night before had been so powerful! The Holy Spirit had given people *gold teeth!* With barely sustainable bewilderment and profound spiritual fatigue, I congratulated her and hung up the phone.

Fifteen minutes later I drove past the worst car accident I have ever seen. A blood-soaked sheet thrown over a body on a gurney, a mess of twisted metal and shattered glass, flashing lights and emergency vehicles clogging up the Los Angeles freeway and slowing traffic down enough to give us each a good, long look at the gory site.

Something inside me finally snapped. Gripping the steering wheel to stop my hands shaking, with my face raised to the windshield, I shouted to the smoggy sky and the Hollywood

Hills, "Fuck you, God! *I'm out!* You can keep your gold teeth! I'm done! If there is to be anything further between us, it's on you!"

The day I gave up on God, I crash-landed into my life with undisguised honesty and fuck-it-all fearlessness. Into the vacuum of my former faith flooded one savage conviction: *God owes us all a giant apology.* Unless God did it all on purpose, in which case God was diabolical, God couldn't have known how bad it would get, how bad we humans could make it. Whichever it might be, if God had any remorse whatsoever, any humanity at all, God had better be sitting and holding the hand of the suffering and dying. Given the seemingly limitless potential for heartbreak and horror in this life, if God was not filled with almighty regret, and prepared to look each one of us in the face when we stand before the throne of glory and say, *Oh, my dear, I am so very sorry*, then I wanted nothing more to do with God. About this I was clear.

While I was learning to preach, Andy was learning to be a theologian. When I would come to a text and not be able to figure out my way in, he would prompt me to ask a particular question of the Scripture. This question, he would remind me, would surely reorient me out of whatever rabbit hole I had gone down trying to figure out what to say and return me to the purpose of the sermon and the Bible itself.

The question, it turns out, is the same one we ask when things get flipped upside down: *Who is this God? And what is God up to here?* (Two questions, really, but Andy never was one for brevity, so let's treat them as one.)

This question has shaped my faith more than any other. I've found that it opens every Scripture passage, because surely every single part of the Bible is trying to say *something* about who God is and trying to show *something* about what God does. Whether it is an account of an ancient battle, a graphic love song, a miracle of Jesus, a pastoral letter to a rowdy community, or apocalyptic poetry, the reason it was told and written down, preserved and canonized, read and preached, is that it tells us something of who God is and what God does.

One text, in particular, is a fascinating study. Psalm 22 is a psalm of David, in which he spells out his utter despair and anguish, with vivid and terrible imagery, and accuses God of abandoning him. It opens with these decidedly accusatory words: "My God, my God, why have you forsaken me?"

It doesn't say, *My God, have you abandoned me?* It says, *Why have you abandoned me? Why are you so far from helping me?*

These are words to make a preacher nervous.

If we're asking this text the questions, *Who is this God, and what is God up to?* then these words suggest that we must begin by accepting that God has forsaken this person, that God, in fact, abandons us. God is sometimes silent to our cries. God is sometimes absent.

In the faith perspective I grew up with, this is heresy. *If you feel like God is absent*, I was told, *it is because you are.* You must search your heart for what is blocking your connection to God. You must find your way back to the faithful God. God is unchanging. God is never absent. We change; we stray. If you think your prayers for help are going unanswered, it is simply that you are not paying attention to the answer. Or perhaps they've been answered in a way you don't like and so refuse to acknowledge.

For the first half of my life, nobody I had known, no pastor or Sunday school teacher or youth leader, no mentor or camp counselor or conference speaker, and not even a regular fellow Christian, would have said, *Yep. God sometimes goes AWOL. Yes, it's a legitimate experience to wrestle with the very real absence of God.*

And yet . . . and yet not only is this question in the mouth of King David, in the prayer book of our Scriptures for all generations of believers before and after Christ to read and pray, but this very prayer was in the mouth of *Jesus himself* as he hung dying on the cross.

And he did not whisper it quietly under his breath, so as not to shake the faith of others. Jesus shouted it from the feeble depths of his suffocating lungs during his crucifixion, to be heard by his executioners and followers alike, his enemies and his admirers. Those who believed he was who he said he was and those who were glad to see him die for his blasphemous claim all heard him wail, *My God, my God, why have you forsaken me?*

So the original question, which was compelling enough to begin with, just got a lot bit juicier. Because if we ask, *Who is God and what is God up to here?* not only is God the one doing the abandoning, but God is, apparently, also the one abandoned, screaming out the accusation against God, *Why have you forsaken me?* Godforsakenness is an experience that God knows intimately in Christ's own human soul and viscerally in his own dying flesh and bones.

I wish I had known this sooner in my life: There is a whole aspect of our faith—going back to its very beginning—that doesn't pretend things are fine when they are not. It doesn't pretend God is near when God is not. It doesn't ask us to pretend that we are OK when we are not—a "dark night of the soul," Saint John of the Cross called it in the sixteenth century. The mystics do not shy away from this kind of faith. And they don't shy away from the "psalms of disorientation," as Walter Brueggemann calls them. These psalms are massive complaint-and-blame bombs directed at the Almighty, for the times when everything you thought was real crumbles, and those "psalms of orientation" that praise God's trustworthy goodness and life's good order no longer work for you.

What time had I ever spent with the psalms of disorientation? In all my years of Christianity, and as an insider of church life, when had I ever read all the way through this particular psalm, without skimming past the drama of it? I had never let in the deeply embodied, visceral anguish, the dark imagery that resorts to metaphor to communicate such deep despair and the soul torment of total abandonment and absolute desolation.

This is in our Bible. This *is our Scripture.* There are prayers in our Bible that articulate feeling completely cut off from God, from others, from your very self, with no agency, just helpless dejection, watching your life disappear before your eyes while God lifts not a finger to stop it.

The fact that this Scripture was cried out *by Jesus himself* as he hung dying tells me two things that I wish I had known in my own dark night of the soul.

1. It's OK to feel this way. To suffer in this way and tell God and even tell whoever will listen is a valid human experience.

2. To have this Scripture, this prayer, at the ready gave Jesus comfort. God incarnate was able to reach for these words, to cry out these words, because they were available to him. When he felt like this (*he felt like this!*), he knew he could draw from words written generations before and prayed throughout his childhood by his community. *When we feel this way, we cry out to God.*

What a gift is available to us that we do not grab hold of!

What is God up to? If God's goal in coming as Jesus was to save us all from our sin and sadness and give us promises of triumph and guarantees against pain and misery, then for Jesus to cry this out while he is dying is dreadfully undermining to his whole message. How humiliating and damaging it is to declare to the whole world that you were wrong all along—that in the end, God wasn't there for you after all but that God abandoned you!

But if Jesus's message is that absolute connection to God and to each other is possible—is, in fact, what we are already given by God—so that I can take even my anger at God (!), even my abandonment by God (!), even my very accusations and disappointment over God's apparent lack of care (!), and I can shout it all at God (!!), even in front of other people (!!), and it cannot end things between us (!!!), it cannot stop God from being God or me from belonging to God (!!!!), then what a powerful moment of truth this is.

God seems to be saying, *I cannot enter in and be fully human until I have also experienced completely what it is to be cut off from God, to be lost, to be alone and afraid, hopeless and helpless.* And then Jesus does just that: Jesus dies. As theologian Jürgen Moltmann often reminds us in his writing, God experiences death from both sides: the triune God knows what it is to die and knows what it is to lose a child to death. Death enters into the Trinity itself and separates what cannot be separated. Death and loss—of the family, of community, of relationships that make you who you are—are something God knows *firsthand.*

Jesus cried out accusations against God from the cross. The very real experience of godforsakenness is paradoxically the very place God meets us.

If we are working hard to prop up our faith and correct our attitude, adjust to our circumstances with a cheerful disposition, and stuff down or avoid any anguish we may feel, if we are trying to get through the godforsakenness by pretending to be OK when we are not OK, we are missing God right where God is—on the cross, bearing our suffering with and for us.

When we let go of trying to preserve God's reputation, and our own status as "faithful," and come instead to a place of utter honesty, *there* God can be near to us, *there* God can find us. We might be sad, we may be scared, but we're not alone.

When I lost home and family, all the belonging I had known and the structures that made life make sense—when all I thought I could trust fell apart—something gaping and broad opened up in me. The truth is, though I had certainly known pain and loss, I had never really reached the end of my rope, not really. I had not ventured to the depths of all misery and honesty with God and absolutely let go without hedging my bets. Even my begging for Jenny's healing, in retrospect, had kept a respectful, if insistent, tone.

But now, for the first time in my life, I was not in control. For the first time, I did not filter my feelings through my mind, through others' perceptions, through my beliefs and my principles and correctness. I just let go. I threw it all on God, threw it back to God. I yelled obscenities at God and told God that I had lost all respect for God and that as far as things between God and me went, I was done. I broke up with God. God had forsaken me. God had forsaken all of humanity, I decided, by allowing such suffering to beset us all. God was not to be trusted.

Not long after that freeway drive, I went on a whitewater rafting trip. For nearly ten years, a group of women who had been in youth group together (before it all fell apart) had gathered from wherever in the country we were each living and repeated the whitewater rafting trip we had enjoyed in high school. Each year we grew more and more different from each other, shaped by our diverse life experiences and circumstances. But every year we came together again in Wisconsin for three days to camp in tents, eat lukewarm pudding cups, and raft down the Wolf River.

We were well into our second day of rafting, having pulled over to the side of the river for lunch and then relaunched our boats, relaxing, laughing, and catching up on each other's lives and stories through a calm stretch of water. As we approached the next stretch of rapids, we untied our boats from one another, strapped on our life vests, and picked up our oars to traverse the raging water. This year the river was especially high—so high and fast, we learned later, that the locals were avoiding it. But we didn't know this, and we headed into this stretch of rapids as we had done countless times before.

As soon as we entered the rapids, we began struggling to maintain control of our boats. As we plunged forward and reared up on a wave, I was thrown from my boat into the swirling water. The rapids sucked me under and thrust me to the surface for a moment, where I gasped a breath of air before being thrust under again. Each time my face came out of the water, I could hear my friends yelling my name. My legs and arms crashed against rocks as the river swept me forward, flipping me and tossing me. I wondered if I would die. I wondered if I would lose my engagement ring. These were the only two thoughts I remember having. They felt of equal importance.

Finally, I was able to jam my foot between two rocks and pull my head out of the water. I watched the boats race past me with my friends screaming words of encouragement.

I was wedged in, a few feet from a large rock in the middle of the river, and only about sixty yards from the end of the stretch of rapids. I inched forward and grabbed on to the rock and pulled myself on top of it. The last boat approached, but before the river carried it past my rock, my friend Lana jumped from her boat into the rapids. She struggled over to the rock where I sat—shivering and scraped, bleeding and crying—and she scrambled up next to me. She hugged me, and then she sat with me for a very long time. We watched the other boats pull to the side of the river at the end of the rapids and saw our friends climb out to wait on the banks of the river.

Sixty more yards of churning water roiled between us and them, and I was paralyzed. With no guarantees in life except for death, and God an unknown entity, the fear I felt was different from the fear I'd felt at any other point in my life. I was angry with God, frustrated with God, confused about God, and I'd pretty much shown God the door. I really did not know if I could pray, on many levels. Was praying to make it to the shore like praying for a parking spot? Did God care about something as trivial as me, scared, in the middle of a river, when people were really suffering elsewhere? (God hadn't stepped in to stop that suffering.) Could I pray now, in a time of need, when I was avoiding God otherwise?

It turned out that I couldn't bring myself to pray. The energy and trust it would take me to even address God directly were completely depleted. My faith was all but dead. My trust in God had gone a long time without oxygen. But I knew that Lana, sitting next to me, still had faith.

So I turned and asked her, "Will you please pray?" She nodded and looked out over the water and asked God to help us. Then we stood up, grabbed hands, and jumped into the river.

When I had raged at God, no holds barred, I had *no idea* this kind of back talk was such a legitimate part of faith, that *Jesus himself had done likewise*. And when I'd left my life raft of a fiancé to go whitewater rafting with the girls and ended up staring death in the face, I was not alone. Lana took my hand and jumped into the raging water with me. She shared my place. Her faith was enough for both of us. She leaped from her boat into the water and crawled up on the rock next to me. But it wasn't just Lana there beside me; it was Jesus himself.

Even as I was wrestling with the very real absence of God, Jesus was there holding my hand. And Jesus had been alongside me in the car on the freeway that day too, lending me his own words as I shouted about the lives snuffed out on the asphalt outside my window. *God, why have you forsaken me? Why have you forsaken us all?*

These are ancient words. In that moment, when Jesus shouts these words from the cross, not only does godforsakenness get taken up into God, but the imagination of every God-fearing person who overhears him ignites and recalls praying this psalm throughout their own lives, as their ancestors did before them.

Time slows down and folds in on itself into timelessness. Vast and beyond comprehension, the intimate words prayed by King David a thousand years before must have risen up in the onlookers' memories, as Jesus Christ embodied this psalm: *My God, my God, why have you forsaken me! . . . I can count all my ribs, my mouth sticks to my jaws, they laugh and mock, they stare and gloat over me, they cast lots for my clothing . . .*

But here's what is so marvelous about all of this—about the whole damn thing of it. Psalm 22 does what many of the psalms of disorientation do: it turns the corner back to trust. It becomes a "psalm of new orientation." Inexplicably, and quite suddenly, it shifts from helpless, abject despair and blame to effusive praise and thanksgiving, empowered trust, and sheer delight. So as Jesus cried out the first line of this psalm, his body wasting away under the crude sign, "King of the Jews," their memories must have recalled the rest of the prayer:

> All the ends of the earth shall remember
> > and turn to the Lord;
> and all the families of the nations
> > shall worship before him.
> For dominion belongs to the Lord,
> > and he rules over the nations.

> To him, indeed, shall all who sleep in the earth bow
> > down;
> > before him shall bow all who go down to the
> > > dust,
> > and I shall live for him.
> Posterity will serve him;
> > future generations will be told about the Lord,
> and proclaim his deliverance to a people yet
> > unborn,
> > saying that he has done it. (Ps 22:27–31)

In the paradox of a godforsaken and supposedly failed savior being put to death in front of them, a new kingdom is simultaneously breaking forth that precedes an ancient, praying poet-king and extends beyond generations yet unborn, past boundaries of peoples, nations, and families, to embrace every person who sleeps in the whole earth. There is no death—of self, or dream, or family, or future, or even of our mortal body—stronger than the life and love of God. We need not fear. We will fear, but we need not. And when we do, we can yell that out to God too. Because there is nothing, *nothing*, that we cannot say to God. And there is no experience so dark, so terrible, so godforsaken that God does not bear it with us.

Who is this God, and what is God up to? Always this. Always here. Always alongside us, even in our godforsakenness. Always at work in the midst of death to bring new life. We don't get to witness what resurrection looks like when it is happening, to see that mysterious mechanism that shifts the psalms of our lives from disorientation to new orientation. Just as we don't get to see what goes on when the dead Jesus's body comes back to life, when the story moves from a detailed account of his death to the inexplicably empty tomb, and suddenly the living, breathing Lord is walking among his friends and disciples. It's not something we can grasp, this life-out-of-death thing. It's mystery, transcendence, something outside ourselves that we cannot muster up or break down.

There are no steps we take to have life resurrected within us. Only openness and honesty and waiting with our hands outstretched (or even clenched tightly shut). Because resurrection is not something we do, it's the Holy Spirit's work. It is God—this same God we've accused of abandoning us—who, when all is said and done, brings redemption and life and hope.

In the very, very end, life and love win, no matter what. And this is true even now. If we let ourselves be where Jesus is, in the raw realness of our lives, God *will* do this. God will bring life out of the death of us. God will bring hope out of the despair of us.

I couldn't have realized it at the time, and I certainly didn't feel it at the time, but what felt like apostasy, my own abandonment of God, was the place where God would meet me. The death of my faith was the precursor of my resurrection.

Right around the time my parents got divorced, my new fiancé's parents got divorced too. Surprise! Andy and I found ourselves planning a wedding in the fresh carnage of our parents' marriages, both of which were ending after nearly twenty-five years. The existential torment was so great that we spent every extra cent we had on counseling, both individually and together, and told our therapists, *No secrets! Share anything that concerns you from one of our sessions with the other person, please!*

We struggled with belonging, even with *being. We are not children*, we told ourselves. *Divorce shouldn't be impacting us so severely.* And yet it was. If the origins of our being, our very selves and our identity as people, came from unions that never should have been, it's as though we ourselves never should have been. (Andy eventually even wrote a book about the ontological effects of divorce on the offspring.)[1] To be planning a marriage together in the midst of all this felt ridiculous and foolhardy. It also felt brave, filled with some kind of hopeful defiance—a necessary act of survival, even.

During all this, I wasn't sure what to do about my dad. I had tried to continue our conversations, but even in the "coming clean" of his secrets spilling out, he continued to lie to me. This felt utterly inconceivable. My dad had been infallible, invulnerable, only goodness and wisdom personified; that this was not entirely so was a short circuit to my system. In order to reorient my own self in the world—to learn to trust my own observations and instincts instead of defaulting to him as the arbiter of all—I stopped speaking to him. I didn't know how else to find my true north.

My conundrum about my dad came to a head when I walked into the seminary bookstore one morning. It had been more than six months since we had talked, and there, prominently on display, was one of my dad's books advertised for an upcoming class in the doctor of ministry program. My heart started racing. Did I have a responsibility to say something to someone about him and how "far he'd fallen"?

I felt paralyzed, at a standstill in my relationship with him as the public figure and with him as my dad. I had no clear idea of, or even desire for, a way forward. But this couldn't go on forever because just three months away loomed the big question: Would my dad walk me down the aisle?

I took my quandary to one of my professors, Ray Anderson. I knew he knew who my dad was; I'd seen my dad mentioned in a footnote in one of Ray's books. But I also somehow knew he wouldn't be devastated when he heard about my family's situation, like the counselor in Kansas City my sisters had sought help from. They had realized their error when they sat down and noticed all of my dad's books lined up in the center of the shelf behind the man's desk. (The realization was reiterated when, at the news of our family's demise, he wept in front of them.)

I sat across from Ray in his comfortably cluttered office, with piles of books teetering on the table and the edge of the desk near me. Ray planted a chair across from me and sat down. I poured out my story. He received me with a kind and steady gaze. He did not flinch or grimace; he only listened with care. And then he spoke. "People in shame don't believe they deserve anything," he said. "Your dad doesn't believe he deserves to walk you down the aisle. You are in a unique position to show your dad *grace*. This is a public, defined role with clear boundaries. It requires little from you in terms of letting him in, where you may not be ready to share personal things. Five years from now, when all of this is no longer fresh, what will you wish you had done?"

I felt the gift of his words seep into my soul. *He made me feel like I had a calling.* In my weakness, he saw me as a minister. Ray gave me a glimpse beyond the pain and betrayal to the larger truth of my belonging and my dad's—to God, to each other. He helped me see a small way to stay attached to that reality, even in the midst of such disintegration and fracture. Without realizing I needed it, I stepped into a participation role. I saw I had a choice to join in God's healing, to be part of what God might be doing in my dad, even if I wasn't ready to move toward him myself. By inviting me to show grace to my father, Ray showed me grace. I didn't grasp its significance at the time, but in the midst of my pain and confusion, by seeing me as a minister and inviting me to see myself that way too, Ray gave my soul a way to stay rooted in the deepest belonging.

As to the rest of the wedding, to navigate the minefield of drama between ourselves and our two dissolving families, our wedding weekend was scripted down to the minute. We choreographed family gatherings around meals, events, and territories as if we were the New York City Ballet. I wrote a brutally honest wedding service, relying heavily on Episcopalian liturgy and scripted responses that were completely foreign to my Evangelical upbringing and unlike weddings anyone in my tradition had attended, unless they had witnessed the vows of some Catholic neighbor's kid. No bombastic pastoral personalities, no mushy self-revealing vows, no off-the-cuff prayers. We were going to use the words spoken by people for thousands of years; who cares if they weren't *our* people.

I also wrote a whole theological paper on my philosophy of marriage (I read many books to prepare for this), including the meaning of each element of the service, which we gave to our accommodating and patient officiants with strict instructions not to deviate in any way whatsoever from the content or theology therein. My three sisters sang a song written by Erin at my request: "I would like you to write a song about how life is filled with pain and suffering, and how we can't trust in anything, and in the end, God is going to apologize to all of us, because God didn't know how bad it would be." She touched on some points but skirted the goal, and the song included the line, "In the end we will say it had been worth it all." She tells me that afterward I said to her, "I doubt it. It's a beautiful song, and I love it, thank you. But I seriously doubt that."

Disillusioned, with our lives in upheaval, but also in love and feeling the strength of standing together in our weakness, Andy and I began our marriage in survival mode, holding hands in the rapids, clinging to each other and shutting out family and anything else that might rock our safety.

April 2016–March 2017

Shortly after his diagnosis, Marty told me that he just wanted to make it to spring so he could ride his bike again. And he did, riding his bike all spring and through the summer. He met friends for lunch or dinner almost daily. He walked around the lake every night and continued to do the things that gave him joy—mainly, being with others. Even as he was definitely dying, he didn't hold back from living.

Told he likely had just a few weeks to live, Marty defied all predictions. A whole year went by. A year in which "tumors too numerous to count" invaded nearly every system and organ in Marty's body. He could now feel several of them from the outside. In addition to the painful bulge behind his knee, there was one in the center of his back that pressed against him when he lay down or leaned back in a chair. They bothered him greatly. Others impeded his breathing, pressed against his bladder, or caused vague, strange pain in his kidneys, pancreas, and liver. Yet on he went, defying the doctor's expectations and living in relatively good health. He continued to tell the truth about his pain, and we continued to listen and bear it with him.

Chapter 5

In the In-Between

I said to my soul, be still, and wait without hope
For hope would be hope for the wrong thing;
    wait without love,
For love would be love of the wrong thing; there
    is yet faith
But the faith and love and hope are all in the
    waiting.
Wait without thought, for you are not ready for
    thought:
So the darkness shall be the light, and the still-
    ness the dancing.

—T. S. ELIOT, *Four Quartets*

Standing on the threshold,
all we've left undone smirking in our periphery,
all we carry with us a finger's breadth away,
    waiting, waiting.
Unfinished business clings heavy, disappointment,

pressure, expectations straining at the seams.
And what we would love to step out of
and leave behind in an unwashed heap on the
     floor
abandoning on tipsy tiptoe, light and free.
It's all right here, balanced, but barely,
on the threshold.

—KARA K. ROOT, excerpt from
"Prayer for a New Year"

*F*or the next several months, Marty was no longer the Marty he had been, living the trajectory he'd laid out for his life, existing within the rhythms of work and play that had defined his days and years. At the same time, what was coming next had not yet arrived. He couldn't step into it in any deliberate way; he merely had to await its arrival. He was marooned on a threshold. "Liminality" comes from the Latin word *limen*, meaning "threshold." Being in a liminal state is like being in a doorway between rooms, an in-between reality character-ized by the loss of capacity to rely on what has been and by complete uncertainty about what will be. This is where Marty was now, paused in this undefined and little-explored place in between living and dying.

Not long after I told God I was throwing in the towel on our relationship, I was awarded the seminary's Parish Pulpit Fellowship for "excellence in preaching and commitment to parish ministry." This meant that some generous anonymous

donors were giving me money to travel and study after graduation. Every year they made a financial investment in the belief
that it would make one smart and lucky student into a better
pastor if they had the chance to supplement what they had
learned in seminary with a broader, experiential education
utterly of their own choosing. I was that year's student.

Even though I felt like the world's hugest hypocrite, I
took the money. This was amazing, and I had no idea what
else to do with my life at the moment. So my new husband
and I packed everything we owned into a fifteen-by-fifteen-
foot storage unit, surrendered our apartment, forwarded our
mail to a PO Box, put our student loans on hold, filled two
backpacks and a duffel bag with just a tad more than we could
carry, and essentially dropped off the grid for six months.

We circumnavigated the globe, heading west. Beginning in Hawaii and Fiji, we dropped anchor in Australia
for three months and then progressed through Egypt and
Israel to Europe, where we bounced around from country to
country, currency to currency, language to language, with
nothing but the packs on our backs, pausing in London, and
eventually returning to Southern California via New York
City. When we left for the trip, we had been married for just
over a year.

We had lost the capacity to rely on what had been and were
completely uncertain about what would be next. And so we
found ourselves in a liminal state. Roaming the world, far
from all we had ever known, I was also newly severed from
everything that had defined me for the previous twenty-four
years of my life. At times the *time* seemed to stretch on forever.

The life I had known in Southern California as a full-time student with a part-time job living at a breakneck pace came to a screeching halt when we boarded that first plane.

God and I had begun making tentative inroads with one another; our relationship felt more honest, less sure, different from before. I had no more plans to go into ministry, and the future was altogether unclear. Except for what I had in my backpack, all my earthly possessions were in storage. My seminary friends had graduated and moved away to start their careers in new places. My childhood home was gone, and my parents were living in strange apartments I had never seen on opposite sides of the country from each other. My rootedness in family, my faith in God's goodness, and my trust in the church—the three things that had most defined and secured my life—were gone. And in the place of all this was . . . nothing. The slate was wiped clean.

That there were no expectations laid on me at all finally sank into my guilty conscience when a seminary representative emailed me a couple of weeks into our trip to say that I didn't need to send so many detailed updates striving to prove to the anonymous donors that I was properly earning their money. I was to just receive and enjoy the experience.

With nowhere I had to be, nothing I had to do, and besides my new husband, nobody I knew or who knew me, I found myself feeling cleared of all clutter and cobwebs and rinsed clean inside. I had nothing to prove, earn, or accomplish, nothing to fight, fix or figure out. Nothing. My old life had just come to a conclusive ending, and a new life had not yet begun. I was between existential planes—dislocated, uncertain. I was in liminality.

After the snorkeling and sunset exhilaration of Fiji and Hawaii, we landed in a flat in Melbourne, Australia. While we were there, Andy was working on his second graduate degree, studying seven hours a day, so I was alone to occupy my bottomless time in a strange city with no connections or routines.

I didn't much trust God when we set out on this journey—and now, when I wasn't distracted by sightseeing or spouse, I was stuck alone with God for hours and hours every day. The experience was existential whiplash. At first I was a terrified, restless mess. It took me three sleepless, agitated, and anxious weeks of wandering the streets of Melbourne in jittery adrenaline detox before I slowed down enough to lift my head and look around and take a deep breath.

I ambled restlessly through busy parks, and when I tired, I would settle into my seat in the small, bright Café Lana with wide windows overlooking the street, my journal open, venting my anxiety and tension in ink, rambling out words until I was settled enough to sit still. And then, on the other side of that, I would feel open and alert. Swept clean inside. I can still remember the feel of the air on the streets of Melbourne, the sound of the streetcars on their rails, and the smell of the eucalyptus trees. I was awake. Present. Coming back into myself, meeting God again. *Who are you, God?*

In this place, I was finally able to simply be. I stopped, and God met me. With written dialogue at times, and simple silence at others, God came back to me as the comforting presence I had known as a child, with a spaciousness to hold all my questions and grief and disillusionment. And God turned my gaze inward as well, slowly reminding me who I was apart from all that I had thought made me strong, or whole, or good, or necessary. God began to heal my broken heart and show me how my very brokenness would become a dark and rich place for new life to grow, the place within me where I would share most deeply in God's life and the life of the world. *Who am I?*

Also on that trip, in our shared, extended liminal state, I discovered Andy and what it was to belong to another person. Rootless and drifting through slow time in close proximity with no bills to pay, errands to run, or calls to return, we belonged to no community and were near no family or friends, or acquaintances of any kind, really. We had each other, and we had relentless, unstructured, uninterrupted time. We learned how to live with each other. We learned how to share. We learned how two introverts can coexist: how to respect each other's space and how to find space for ourselves in unfamiliar terrain. We learned how to budget, down to the penny, how to keep track of expenses and juggle plane tickets and train tickets and meals on a set amount that needed to stretch around the globe.

We discovered that most of our fights would happen when we'd gone too long without food and that fatigue often comes out as anger. Without alarm clocks or obligations, we learned our own and each other's sleep rhythms and most productive times of day, and we discovered just how much capacity we each had for adventure and ancient ruins before we'd need a Big Mac and an internet cafe. We learned who was better with the map and who was better with train timetables and how to tell each other over someone's head with just a look that *no, this hostel is not where we want to stay and, yes, I'm right behind you if you bolt for the door.*

Through seasickness, homesickness, heartsickness, choking boredom, tons of laughter, more than a few tears, and endless miles of *literally* walking side by side, we learned things about life together in relationship that would have taken us years to figure out if the lessons had been diluted with jobs, friends, study schedules, utility bills, and all the joys and struggles of ordinary life. But in this intense liminality, these lessons were melded into our being, and our being with each other, deeply and wordlessly, simply by the heat of constant proximity and duration. *Who are we?*

The times in our lives of suffering and loss, wondering where God is and what could possibly be the meaning of all this, are often referred to as "wilderness" experiences. And undeniably, there are lots of ways to explore the wilderness as the place of loss. But I am fascinated by the wilderness as a liminal place, by its function as a threshold, an in-between spot, where both tearing down and building up occur. And I am struck by how often God's movement of us from captivity to freedom—God's invitation to repentance, God's work of salvation—in whatever ways, and for whatever reason, involves spending time in wilderness, with the questions liminality floods us with: *Who is God? Who am I? Who are we?*

In the definitive biblical wilderness experience, the Israelites are led out of slavery in Egypt to cross the Red Sea and head into the long-drawn-out experience of liminality (Exod 1:6–22 and 15:20–16:8). In order to be the people of God, the Hebrews have to first stop being the people of Pharaoh. Just because God sets them free from captivity doesn't mean they are suddenly fundamentally different. They carry their oppression, fear, and mistrust within them. The wilderness is filled with complaining and fear. The urge to self-preservation is intense, the lack of cohesion and unity is palpable, and the distrust of God and their leader Moses is incessant.

They are in this in-between place for forty years. A giant *stop* in their story. Letting go of the old, not yet ready to step into the new—they are existing between two existential planes. Their identity is in suspension, with the death of all they've known behind them and their future yet unborn. They are no longer slaves. They are not yet free. The liminal is their detox, their reset button, their school of identity and purpose. They need to meet God again. They need to meet themselves again. They need to discover each other anew.

The people are going to have to get to know God out here where it is just them and God, face to face, for an extended period of time without any distractions, good or bad. Who they are and where they go from here depend on this. They cannot live as free people in a promised land if they carry their slavery within. They must rely on God and come to trust in God's love and care for them, God's relentless *for*-them-ness, God's *hesed* promise to be a different kind of Lord from the lords they had known in Egypt. They must trust that they belong to God.

When the liminal descends, it might come as a huge, drop-off-the-grid experience or as weary wilderness waiting for a new chapter to begin or for an unexpected loss to propel us into the unknown next. Whenever the stage of in-between arrives, it takes away who we were and withholds for a time who we will become, so the questions that echo all throughout the thresholds and in-betweens can descend to claim their rightful space: *Who is God? Who am I? Who are we?*

For the Israelites, the wilderness is the place of complete dissolution of order as they have known it (and bad as it had been, at least it was order). But new structures are being constructed within them that they do not yet realize. And later on, they will look back and decide that this time—as hard as it is, as disorienting, uncomfortable, confusing, and boring—is the formative experience of their entire corporate existence. They'll one day say that who they are, and how they live together, came from this time.

And even more, this time defines for them who God is. God is not only "the Lord, the God of your ancestors, the God of Abraham, the God of Isaac, and the God of Jacob" (Exod 3:15). Now God says, "I *am* the Lord your God, who brought you out of the land of Egypt, out of the house of slavery" (Deut 5:6; my italics), the God who will continue to care for them, even in the times when the promises are hard to see and the people feel all but forgotten.

And then, throughout the rest of Scripture, and through all of Jewish history, the story of God's provision in the wilderness will become, especially during the exile, a source of great hope and identity. It defines them as a people cared for by God and teaches them how to be this people with each other. And it repeatedly reintroduces them to God who is steadfast, even when we can't see the way, God who provides when it all looks hopeless, God who leads us and never lets us go, even when we doubt and question and test. Remembering their wilderness sustains them through future times of struggle, hopelessness, and the unknown. This *stop* that seems to take them out of the story becomes instead the fulcrum of the whole thing.

After six months of wandering, Andy and I came home—which is to say, we brought home with us and set it down in one place. It took us all of eighteen hours from the time our plane touched down to find an apartment in Pasadena and sign a lease. And by the end of the weekend, we were moved in completely, every picture on the wall and sock in its drawer, and we were filling out job applications—so eager were we to begin the next phase of our lives.

Gradually, imperceptibly, in that liminal space of travel, I had been healing, changing, settling into myself. When we returned, I was surprised to discover that I now knew who I was and where I was going. It was on this trip that I realized that I still, and deeply, loved the church and that I could not live without it. My purpose was tied up in it, and I knew I was going to come back and be a pastor.

We came home and surrendered our patchwork religious backgrounds and became Presbyterian. The emphasis on God's sovereignty, the way we trust that God chooses us before we can choose back, the "reformed and always in need of being reformed" all spoke to us. Andy's liminal confirmation was that he would pursue a PhD and go on to teach, so he began studying for the GRE and applying to grad schools. Individually and together, we had a sense of our future and a sense of how our past had shaped and prepared us for what was to come.

Like the Israelites in the wilderness, I found that the liminal was my detox, my reset button, my school of identity and purpose. I needed to meet God again. I needed to meet myself again. I needed to discover my place of belonging with and for another again. *Who is God? Who am I? Who are we?* My faith had been shattered and rebuilt. The destruction of my world as I had known it, and the discovery of God's world with me in it, became the defining experience of my life trajectory. The liminal was my place of rebirth.

Marty's liminality, by contrast, was a place of predeath. For all intents and purposes, his life had ended. There was no looking forward beyond the next day or hour. His future consisted of the next procedure, nap, or lunch date. His threshold was between the life he had known and the foregone conclusion of death.

And yet believing he had only weeks left to live, and instead living well past that time in a suspended state of relatively good health for months on end, meant he was "in the world but not of it"—he was among us, but not of us. He found a way to let go and live so completely on the threshold, so fully in the moment, that his most prominent emotion was gratitude. Marty was living on borrowed time, so every minute was a gift. Gratitude allowed him to exist in that space between living and dying, somehow fully doing both.

In some way, he had met himself again. He was living in touch with, and guided by, his deepest desires, his joy, his primary belonging to God and to others. Grace surrounded every step of his journey. Marty was bathed in grace. This should not be surprising, since the first grace the human being ever knows is our creatureliness itself, our embodied, fragile mortality. In the creation story in Genesis 1–2, we are reminded that we are creatures connected to the earth, living inside bodies that are trapped inside the confines of time and space. And it is from within these vulnerable bodies, from within these confines of time and space, that God's grace encounters us. First and foremost, human beings are creatures in need of our Creator's care. I imagine when we feel acutely the confines of our own mortality, as Marty did, living so tuned in to the functions and dysfunction of our mortal body, we are nearer to the truth of grace. Intense awareness of our creatureliness, coupled with a profound experience of dependence upon the Creator and the attentive care of others, returns us completely to our belonging to God and each other. It immerses us in grace.

Our truest and deepest self already knows being loved and claimed by God. This reality is already ours; it is the gift we have been given with our very existence. We belong to God. We were made for this dynamic relationship with God and each other called grace. Grace is not something God does; *it's who God is.* God can't not embrace and love us no matter what. God's being spills over onto us, drawing us from the very beginning into relationship with God.

Grace is the preexisting connection between us and God that never ends. And it's available to us right now. Every single *right now*. Like this one. Our most true and fundamental humanity is of rest, not unrest. It is connected to God, not estranged from God. Disorder is a disruption of what is already the case. We don't imagine that people start out sick and only achieve health from the cure. Sickness is a distortion of health. We start healthy, and then something makes us sick, and the cure restores us to health. So it is with grace.[1] We begin connected to God, then we are separated—by sin and fear and distrust and supposed self-sufficiency—and God reconnects us. As Marty experienced the sickness of his body, the distortion of his physical health, he paradoxically also experienced more poignantly the fundamental order of his being, its rest in the grace of God. His liminal state, his suspended existence—fully present in this life that would soon be gone—was, most of the time, simply a gift.

One of the most significant moments for me in this time was when I got to hear from Marty his whole life story. I typically hear a person's life story from family members after that person has died, while we are preparing for their funeral. I had never before had someone narrate their own life for me. We set a date, and one day Marty came in, sat on a couch across from me, and began. For two hours, I got to revel in the absolute mystery and wonder of discovering someone I thought I knew, through his life laid out before me in his own words. And to my surprise, beneath his ordinary, mild exterior was an entire universe.

A couple of years before, on a church retreat, we had played an icebreaker (often used as a drinking game), "Never have I ever . . ." In the church version, instead of alcohol, each person has a pile of pennies or beads. You say something you've never done that you think several people in the group have done, and everyone who has done that thing puts in a bead. The last one to have any beads left wins. It's a wonderful way to get to know people better, especially those you thought you already knew. The items that bring in the big haul are always surprises like *I've never been on an airplane* or *I've never learned to ice skate* (that Minnesota travesty is mine).

In this particular game, we'd passed all the obvious items and were having to come up with some more creative ones. One man said, "I've never been rejected by my child." Things got a bit strained because this was outside the light and funny tone of the game. So I kept it real by putting in my bead to indicate that my own eight- and five-year-olds had indeed rejected me on more than one occasion. But I also noticed Marty stiffen and a shadow come over him. As far as I knew, he didn't have children. Nevertheless, with no explanation, he put a bead in and then remained withdrawn for the rest of the game.

When Marty sat down to tell me his story, he included this part. It wasn't the biggest part of his story; he had come to terms with it over time and didn't like to dwell on it. But it was part of who he was. Marty had a daughter he hadn't known about for half her life. He first learned of her existence when she was twelve years old. He tried to be in her life after that, but most of his attempts to get to know her were met with rebuffs or demands that he take her places or buy her things. When she was seventeen years old, she turned him away for good. None of his letters or messages after that was ever returned, and eventually he gave up trying to reach out to her.

Marty had never really formed a family of his own. Years later, his short and bitter marriage to a coworker ended quickly, so most of his life he'd lived alone. Over the years he had dated different people but never married again. "I always thought I wanted to be married. I can think of women I should have married but didn't. Sometimes it's like two slow ships passing in the night; circumstances happen, and for whatever reason you move on. I can think of a couple women I would've liked to be married to, and I think we even would've been good together." Marty's parents were both dead, and he was close with his sister. He'd been distant from his brother as an adult, but since his sickness, the two had reconnected.

Marty's twenties had been wild, filled with exploration and escapades, travel and risky adventures. He had been a hitchhiking, drug-loving hippie. "I never did anything *really* crazy," he said sheepishly to his pastor, by way of explanation. "I went up to the line but not over it." I laughed. "You don't need to mention anything about that part at my funeral," he added.

Then he told me a story:

When I was twenty-four I lived for two years in Colombia. I went with people from Minneapolis that I didn't really know, and after a week in Bogotá I split off on my own. It was scary but exciting, a real maturing experience. I knew it was time to come home when I ran out of money. In Miami, I traded in a plane ticket and bought a bus ticket. I had $1.20 left. People on the bus would ask me what I was eating, and when I would tell people I didn't have money for food, they would get me food. I learned one of the most important lessons in life—*people take care of each other.* We really are in this together, and we need to take care of each other.

We talked about people he admired (his uncle Cliff, his high school English teacher who'd told him he was a good writer) and experiences that had impacted him. We noticed big decisions he had made, regrets he had (not many), and things he was proud of. He learned to love nature as a teenager, walking the tree line of fields or through corn-fields hunting grouse and pheasant with his dad, uncle, and cousins. Being in nature helped him sense God's presence. He often felt God near him on the Gunflint Trail in north-ern Minnesota and when he'd go skiing at Lutsen every year, and while scuba diving, which he loved. "I liked to scuba dive the wrecks in Lake Superior and Isle Royale—there are some great wrecks there. You could see forever, and it was hard-core diving, cold." He grinned to think of it. "The best scuba diving I have ever done was off the coast of Galápagos with my Hutch group of friends [friends from Hutchinson, Minne-sota]. The Jacques Cousteau Marine Reef Park was like nothing I've ever seen; it was so special. There were these giant barrel sponges you could go headfirst into."

Marty had trained to be a social worker, but his life went in another direction. He spent many years working in inven-tory for a large grocery company, then he worked in health care administration, and then began grading tests for a large testing company. But on the side, for a long time, he told me, "I was an astrologer. I did horoscopes in the 1970s. I taught myself and was connected to the astrology community. I did tons of private readings through the seventies and into the first half of the eighties. It was fun, really spiritual in one respect. It makes you realize how similar we all are. Astrology helps you get to know people and people get to know themselves. It is part of how I am known in the community, actually." I was gobsmacked; it was so unexpected. (He might as well have told me that in addition to being a test-grader, he was also an astronaut and well known in the community for his missions to Mars.)

"I have always enjoyed people," he said. "I've always enjoyed helping people. Astrology was like that too. I looked at it as preparing me for social work, and it really did; even though I never went that direction, it was a way to help. People would come to me and say, 'I don't know what to do about this broken relationship,' and I would be able to say, 'You might be down now, but there is light at the end of the tunnel. Focus on that.'"

When I asked him about his experiences of God, Marty expanded on his colorful religious past. "When I was with the Wiccan group we would sometimes do rituals, and they'd be in someone's living room or a temple we rented out."

"You can rent out temples?" I interrupted.

"Yes!" he laughed. "We'd do something like drawing down the moon, for example. Anyway, we'd do a banishing in the space first, to drive away the bad and attract the good, and I felt it then. It's the same thing I feel in our sanctuary, the presence of God. When we're really into the service and then we all quiet down inside, I can feel God."

Marty was summing up his life for me. In his liminal state, he was clear that his life as he had known it was over. What was coming for him he had no way of either hurrying up or slowing down. He was relinquishing control of his narrative from this point onward, so it was important to him to be able to articulate what he could, looking back.

In the meantime, he lived day to day, moment to moment. While he existed on bonus time in this suspended state of waiting for death, he sought out the experiences that made him feel alive and present. And we waited with him. Even though our lives continued, we shared his liminality as best as we could.

When he'd come to the end of his life narrative, Marty wrapped up the telling of his story by saying, "I love my church community. I love the synchronicity of giving and receiving; it's been great here. I love all you guys." His eyes sparkled, and he leaned forward. "I have friends who inquire, who say they're agnostic, but they ask me, 'Marty, how's church going? You still at Lake Nokomis?' And I tell them, 'Yes, I love it there!' It's fitting that the end of my spiritual journey is coming here. It was the right thing to do. Like coming home."

Chapter 6

When We Stop

Are you tired? Worn out? Burned out . . . ? Come to me. Get away with me and you'll recover your life. I'll show you how to take a real rest. Walk with me and work with me—watch how I do it. Learn the unforced rhythms of grace. I won't lay anything heavy or ill-fitting on you. Keep company with me and you'll learn to live freely and lightly.

—MATTHEW 11:28–30 MSG

The sun hears the fields talking about effort and the sun smiles, and whispers to me, "Why don't the fields just rest, for I am willing to do everything to help them grow?" Rest, my dears, in prayer.

—SAINT CATHERINE OF SIENA, from Daniel Ladinsky, *Love Poems from God*

Marty's pause in a state of being neither here nor there reintroduced Marty to God who is steadfast, even when we can't see the way, a God of grace, who provides, and leads, and never lets us go. No longer so many of the things Marty had been, he was being redefined almost solely as a person cared for by God, a person deeply connected to others. So, among us and alongside us, Marty lived each day in the grace of his threshold reality.

It has been twenty years since my own epic liminal experience. A few summers ago Andy and I took Owen and Maisy, who by then were twelve and nine, to Australia. We ended up staying in the same apartment in Melbourne that we had lived in years before. It was a surreal experience opening the front door and stepping inside again. The space had changed so little, and we had changed so much. We wandered slowly from room to room reminiscing, to our children's chagrin. The first night we were there, I tucked my son into bed on the couch where I had lain many nights gazing up at the ceiling. When I leaned back and looked up, I gasped. "What is it, Mom?" he asked, concerned.

"I know this ceiling!" I said, with tears in my eyes. He looked at me like I was crazy. I tried to explain all the time spent lying on the couch and staring up at that ceiling meant that *these* cracks in *this* ceiling felt like old friends who'd silently borne witness to my soul's rebirth, smiling down on me again. He rolled his eyes and sighed the sigh of a long-suffering kid of a nostalgic.

Over the next few days, Andy and I walked the streets and showed our kids the sights—the city's and our own. *Here's where we'd jog, here's the store where we got groceries* . . . I sat with them in Café Lana, now remodeled and called by a new name, but with the same view of the park. My heart felt full to bursting. Here I was, a world away and more than their whole lifetime later, returning to the site of my wilderness promised land. They mostly put up with all my wistfulness.

My own liminal adventure twenty years before had been followed by an intense hospital chaplaincy and working in four congregations, each of which had dismantled more delusions about churches and had drawn me deeper into trusting God in their own way. Seven rich years I spent in wonky institutions and broken systems, alongside staggering egos and humble servants, watching institutional amnesia and terrified self-preservation at work. I heard plenty of both damaging theology and lifesaving liturgies. I came to know many dear and earnest followers of Jesus either living with questions and struggles or avoiding them aggressively. And I sampled from my own buffet of stumbles, epiphanies, hiding, and braving before I felt ready to truly pastor from a place of trust in God, or at least to aspire to that.

Right around that time, a little congregation in South Minneapolis called Lake Nokomis Presbyterian Church (LNPC) was finding itself ready to trust too. After three years of rest-less questioning, they spent a year earnestly seeking whether it was time to close their doors and be finished as a congre-gation. When their year was up, they knew God had some-thing else in mind for them; they just didn't know what it was yet. They came away from their "revisioning" process feeling called to be "a beacon of hope and a place of sanctuary." Beyond that, it was a mystery. Not clear on how to move forward and unable to go back, they were in their own liminal space.

When we found each other, we met with a spirit of adventurous curiosity toward whatever future God might lay out in front of us and a deep honesty in who we each were and what we brought to the relationship. I told them I came as a mom and a minister, and both callings were equal. I would not work evenings, except for one night a week, and for the first few months, baby Maisy would come with me to the office. When I asked them how they would describe to a nonchurch neighbor what a pastor does, after a few tentative answers, Gary, who had been in the congregation his whole life, said, "Look, we know how to be the church. We just need a pastor." This was the most deeply assuring thing they could say to me, and deeply truthful too, it turned out.

Not long after I arrived, during my first vacation (and also on the two vacations following that), someone in the congregation died. I had conducted a funeral once before, as a hospital chaplain. But after my first funeral as a parish pastor in a mainline denomination, I made a discovery. Being female and short and appearing younger than I am are not assets when leading a funeral. I found myself having to explain who I was over and over again to skeptical mourners at the funeral home. I didn't fit the image people had of a pastor. This changed significantly, however, with one purchase—a clerical collar.

If there was ever a most visible departure from my child-hood church culture to the one I now inhabit, a clerical collar is it. But as soon as I walked into a room wearing the collar, a certain level of ease entered the situation. Every time I lead a funeral, to earn trust with strangers, I still have to overcome my gender and appearance, but at least there is no question now who is going to lead this service. As a "clerical" distinction, I have not been a fan of the outfit. I believe strongly in the priesthood of all believers. I'm ambivalent about convey-ing that I am somehow other, or more or differently holy. I don't like the sense that I am wearing a uniform in society that carries any additional authority or requires specific recogni-tion. We are all ministers; we all do the work of the church. But I've come to appreciate that there are certain times when I need to be seen as carrying some additional authority and to be easily recognized. So I think of it as my "funeral collar." It only comes out of the closet for funerals, for interfaith events, or for public protests when I am there in representation of "the faith," as a stand-in for the church, and for those rare hospital visits when I may not know the person well and need to provide reassurance of my role: *she's here as the pastor.*

When we came together, the people of LNPC and I spent nine months in a process of listening and discernment that first sought to celebrate, grieve, and let go of who they'd been in the past while also recognizing and embracing who they were now. They were pining after the days when they could take big youth mission trips and build Habitat for Humanity homes, comparing themselves to who they used to be or to the churches around them that had impressive youth groups or extensive children's programming, wondering what they had to offer and where they would go.

Instead of focusing on *How can we get back to what we used to be?* or *How can we be like that other church?* together we began asking ourselves the more powerful question of discernment I had learned to ask of Scripture: *What is God up to here?* We sought to pay attention and notice: *Where is God already working in us?* We ventured boldly into those delicious questions of liminality, right where fear and faith collide: *Who is God? Who are we? What is God doing in us right now? And how do we join in more fully?*

This set us free. It takes a lot of pressure off when you say, and really believe, *This is God's church, not ours. And God is already doing something here.* This is not our church to maintain, our ministry to build, our project to do, or our legacy to pass on. This is God's ministry. God is always already at work. My training in spiritual direction gave me this foundation, this trust that God is already and always doing something and that our job is to pay attention to what God is doing and join in. That's it. That's our only job. The church belongs to God. It is God's ministry. And we are all ministers.

This is a brave thing to say in a time when it appears that the church, as we've known it in the West, is dying. Anxiety and fearful predictions about the future of the institution are rampant. Denominations are on shaky ground, congregations are shrinking and drying up, and fewer and fewer people associate with mainline churches in a committed way. More than a decade ago, when Lake Nokomis and I were just getting to know each other, this phenomenon was less pronounced than it is now. Today many congregations that have not yet closed their doors are on the brink of doing so.

New and innovative strategies to "save your church" are aggressively marketed to tired pastors and congregations stretched thin. But at LNPC, we feel clear that this is not our ministry to save. Live or die, we belong to God. So we are free to be whom God has called us to be and leave the survival question to God. It would be hard to overstate the power of feeling free in this way.

Our discernment process brought up three words around which our congregational life is now shaped: *worship, hospitality,* and *Sabbath.* Before I joined them, they'd identified *worship* as their primary purpose. Being in the presence of God together, learning, growing, praising, praying—this is central to this congregation's identity.

Hospitality arose not from some kind of scone-wielding, coffee-urn imagery but because these people knew how to care for each other. They were practiced at welcoming one another and seeing each other as human beings. They'd had a long history as a social justice–oriented congregation that saw themselves as open and welcoming to all. But some of the work we did began to raise the uncomfortable question, *Are we only welcoming and open to those we see as welcoming and open? Are we, in fact, closed and judgmental to those we see as closed and judgmental?* And as often happens when we are willing to look honestly at ourselves and hold ourselves up before God, the questions shifted. They became, *What would it look like to actually welcome all? What would it look like to mutually encounter every person we cross paths with as though we truly belong to them and they to us? And what would it look like to welcome the whole of us—all of ourselves, leaving nothing at the door? How might we be called to deepen our hospitality?*

Sabbath, our third word, was not initially on our radar. It surprised us, piggybacking on *worship* before we embraced it front and center. We'd thought about creativity in worship, different kinds of worship experiences, and what it might look like to loosen our worship schedule to allow for more involved preparation for interaction in our services. Somewhere in the midst of all our brainstorming, we picked up Wayne Muller's book *Sabbath: Restoring the Sacred Rhythm of Rest and Delight*, and the whole congregation began reading it and talking about it in adult education class.

I had the book with me one day while I was staying at a retreat center run by Franciscan nuns. Over lunch, the mother superior mentioned Sabbath to me as central to their calling. I soon learned that the same order of sisters ran a retreat house in the city—just a mile or two from our church building—called "Sabbath House." They offered space for people to come and rest, read, nap, or meet, with lunch if desired. And a couple times a year, they offered a "Sabbath Retreat" day. It was coming up the following month. So several of us attended a first retreat, and then more of us attended a second one. There we learned from a Jewish woman the meaning of Sabbath.

Sabbath is an identity marker, she told us. To be the people of God means to be people who live in God's command to rest—that is, people who are reminded over and over again, every single week, that God is God and we are not. By stopping every week on purpose, we acknowledge that there is nothing we can't set down and step away from. In fact, the urgency and control that keep us constantly in the driver's seat are lies. Life is about something other than doing work and measuring our worth. Sabbath is time dedicated on purpose for no activity other than to dwell in our own lives and let God meet us there. It reorients us to reality.

The Jewish day begins at sundown, she explained. All creativity, invention, and construction happen in the second half of the day, fueled by and resulting from rest. And when the Sabbath day arrives, everything stops, whether we are ready or not. Sabbath interrupts and takes over. We don't start Sabbath after all the work is done, the house is clean, the thank-you notes are written, and the gutters are cleared. When the sun hits the horizon, we stop. The phone goes off, the screens go dark, the work is put down, and the only thing left is human beings being human, in the presence of God, who was there all along but who largely went unnoticed until now.

As she spoke, I was first jealous. This felt revolutionary. I felt shocked that for millennia people had been doing this thing all around me that kept them connected to God and rooted in reality in such a profound way and that I had not really even thought about it. But this rhythm, this stopping regularly, intentionally, choosing it rather than life thrusting a stop upon us, this felt huge.

I began to see that my heart, so drawn to the experience she was describing, already recognized the truth of what she was saying, because it was familiar to me. Every time I had stopped, dwelled in my own life, I'd been reoriented to God. In fact, this stopping seems to be one way God works with me. God pulls me completely out of the life I think I'm living and gives me a liminal experience, a giant pause, a chance to return to myself with God. Some people are good at knowing what they are feeling in the moment, processing experiences as they go. I am not one of these people. I need to get away, get out of a situation, set it down and look back at it, in order to catch up with myself and look for God's presence again.

I had been "Sabbathing" without realizing it. My weekly time in coffee shops with my journal was Sabbath. My time-outs, the chosen ones and the ones that happened against my will, were also Sabbath. My soul already knew something of the importance of turning off and stepping out to get grounded again, to regain perspective on who I am, and am not, in the big picture. I am a person cared for by God and deeply connected to others. I forget this when I don't stop. When I do stop, I remember.

In stark contrast to the world around us—the relentless pace, the endless self-gratification, the frantic climbing and urgent, nonstop work—here was a gift of rest and perspective that was already part of our faith, just not one we'd paid attention to before.

Excitement grew among us. We had been captivated by the concept of Sabbath. There were traces of Sabbath as a cultural practice still in our community—a few people who didn't go shopping on Sundays or who saw Sundays as the time for a big family meal and a nap—remnants from a bygone era by when all of America stopped on "church days." We could see how a rhythm of intentional stopping might be a gift we could offer to others. We could see how Sabbath was meant to be part of a rhythm for us.

We began to learn how to trust in God's perspective through the gift of stopping. We decided to alternate our worship services, designating two Sundays every month as Sabbath days and meeting for worship those weeks on Saturday evenings instead. It took us a while to find our groove and figure out how these services should go, but we finally got there. On those weekends now we gather in a candlelit sanctuary and with many modes of prayer. Using such things as a labyrinth, a giant world map, and prayer practices shaped around coloring, writing, movement, art, and music, we stop, and we set aside the whole next day for stopping. And when we stop, God meets us.

A one-year experiment became a new way of being, and we are now in our thirteenth year.[1] It surprised us and changed us and continues to do both. We struggle with it; some of us really don't like it, mainly because we miss a weekly Sunday-morning service. To others of us who came to the congregation after the shift to this rhythm and the contemplative Saturday worship that sets up the following Sunday as a day of rest, it feels nothing short of life-saving. Throughout all of this, we keep trying to practice listening, and loving, and growing alongside each other. And as we do, the trust deepens and the courage builds to seek God and share life some more.

Who are we? Who is God? What is God up to right here and now? Thirteen years ago, when my congregation sank into these questions together, we put *worship, hospitality,* and *Sabbath* front and center. You might say *worship* is remembering our belonging to God. *Hospitality* is practicing our belonging to each other. And *Sabbath* is returning to our belonging to God and to each other as the ground of our being.

Years before, on that Los Angeles freeway, when I'd let go of my faith and thrown the ball into God's course, maybe for the very first time, I stopped. When I had said to God, *I'm out*, and walked off the court, I unwittingly entered Sabbath time. By letting go of expectations, even hopes, goals, and long-held beliefs, I joined my life already in progress. Gradually, through my long time out, I learned that God is already right here. When we stop, God will meet us. Maybe not the God we thought God was, or the God we wish God were. But the real one. Alive and waiting. Right here. This is where the possibility for new life begins. Letting go of God is where the possibility for new life began for me. Letting go of their future as a congregation is where the possibility of new life began for LNPC.

The Israelites in their wilderness liminal state, having been delivered from slavery but not yet in the promised land, had to be redefined as the children of God instead of the property of Pharaoh. The Israelites were no longer slaves, no longer owned by a master and locked into a system that dictated their worth solely by what they produced. They had lived this way for some four hundred years; it was deep in their psyche. Now they were free, and they would need to learn how free people live, alongside other free people. When God met them in their liminal wilderness, God gave them the

Ten Words, or Ten Utterances, that we know as the Ten Commandments. These are descriptions of life with God in charge instead of Pharaoh. *Here is how a free people live . . .* , God says. And then God speaks the Ten Utterances. Hinged between the Words that describe being people who belong to God (the first three commandments) and the Words describing what it is to be people who belong to each other (the last five commandments) comes this one: "Keep the Sabbath." It is the longest and most detailed Word. Sabbath is the utterance that restores us to personhood.

One day in seven, God says, *you stop all work*. You do this because you are not to be defined by your output. One day in seven everyone rests, and all distinctions that you erect to define your value and measure your worth disappear. Old, young, rich, poor, slave, free, citizen, foreigner—you are all simply and completely human beings, alongside one another, all beloved children of God.[2]

This is the hardest lesson to absorb, so we have to practice it regularly, God tells us. We have to regularly step out of the mindset and activity of the world around us, the measuring, comparing, competing, striving, producing, and consuming. We have to regularly stop *doing* and practice just *being*. As all the other creatures and the earth itself already do, we must surrender to the cycles of rest and renewal that God built into the fabric of existence, which we are passionately determined to circumvent.

One day in seven, this Word says, those who belong to God on purpose remember that we are not God. And God's people on purpose remember that we are neither better nor worse than anyone around us, but connected in a mutual belonging to God and each other. This is what it means to be human. This is what it means to be free. But we forget this most of the time.

While we seek meaning from our lives, the forces of capitalism and progress around us seek to shape how we find that meaning. Constant connectivity in our pockets ensures we're saturated with messages that strip us of our freedom and humanity and suck us into relentless comparison and division, ranking and judging, striving and measuring. With social media, texting, email, and phones ever at the ready, we're justified in acting as though the world can't run without us. (The average American checks their phone eighty times a day *while on vacation*. For that matter, more than half of Americans don't even *take* all their paid vacation days.)[3] We function as though we are separate, independent creatures running on nonstop treadmills of work, forgetting our essential belonging to God and to each other.

Meanwhile, we're so disconnected from our true selves that we can barely stand when emotion of almost any kind arises—it throws off our equilibrium. We're chronically over-committed, underresourced, and exhausted, and who in the world has *time* for Sabbath? If we step off the spinning carousel, it will all fall apart; we're just sure of it. And we'll never figure out how to put it together again. So maybe we label Sabbath self-indulgent, or reserve rest as a reward for a job well done, or see "taking breaks" as a necessary evil in our quest to be more productive. We bolster our Protestant work ethic with a good dose of self-effacing pride. "How are you?" we ask each other. "Busy!" we answer, holding our busyness out like a badge of honor, proof of a life well lived. *Look how well we are producing and consuming! We are not wasting any time.*

But what happens when the mechanism by which you measure your life disappears? What happens when you lose the ability to produce or the means to consume? What happens when you're marooned on a threshold, like the one between living and dying? When all the illusions of strength and self-sufficiency melt away, and you're stuck with your vulnerable old self, just as you are? When you have no control over your own time, and all you can do, by societal measures, is waste it?

By the time Marty got sick, we'd been practicing Sabbath together for five years, and he'd been with us for two of those years. We had reminded each other over and over that Sabbath is one of God's big ten, right up there with *not murdering*, because unless we regularly stop, we forget. We forget that we are creatures—with bodies and minds and hearts that need tending. We forget we are dependent on the love and care of a Creator who is ready to meet us when we stop moving long enough to be met. We forget that we are in this together, alongside everyone else, and that we need one another because life isn't meant to be done alone and against. And human beings who forget their humanity are arguably the most destructive force in the universe.

Rest is not a reward to be earned. It's the starting point. It's uncomfortable, we've discovered. It's strange. We are trained to measure the worth of a day by what we accomplish. So what do we do with a day in which the goal is not to accomplish a thing? We've learned to expect restlessness.

Often there are tears, as emotions we've stuffed down come up in the space we've made. These become, like hunger pangs during a fast, a sacrifice back to God and a gift to us. Tears remind us of our pressing need to stop, revealing in the pain how unaccustomed we have become to being present to our own basic humanity.

When Marty's humanity was in his face every day, all day long, his life became a testimony to the deepest belonging. To God. To each other. Marty was deprived of the chance to try to earn his worth in the traditional ways we do that. What was done was done; he would produce and contribute no more to the world to prove his worth. He just had to accept it. Accept his worth. Accept the love. Accept his intrinsic connection to all others. Accept the time that was given to him, and be present in it just as he was.

"How are you?" we'd ask him. He no longer answered, "Busy." Instead, he told the truth about how he was. Instead, we heard about his real joy and his real pain. And hearing about his real humanity slowed us down to see and embrace our own.

The dignity and beauty of a human being have nearly nothing to do with what we think they do. Our beauty and dignity are given to us by virtue of being alive, created by God, loved by our Creator and connected to all the beings around us. This is what Sabbath had been teaching us; this is what we were learning again through Marty.

Chapter 7

To Move Us from Fear to Trust

———◆———

We know nothing until we know everything. I have no object to defend for it is of equal value to me. I cannot lose anything in this place of abundance I found. If something my heart cherishes is taken away, I just say, "Lord, what happened?" And a hundred more appear.

—SAINT CATHERINE OF SIENA, from
Daniel Ladinsky, *Love Poems from God*

"We seek to be a 'beacon of hope' and a 'place of sanctuary,' to reach out to the needs of neighbors, sharing our selves and our resources"—a safe place to doubt and explore, to participate and connect, to follow Christ and join in God's love and healing of the world.

—LAKE NOKOMIS PRESBYTERIAN CHURCH,
expansion of the Vision Statement (2007)

I won't go to sleep tonight unless you have spoken to me those words that you read to yourself when you need comfort, God.

—SAINT TERESA OF AVILA, from Daniel Ladinsky, *Love Poems from God*

When Marty wandered in and wormed his way into everyone's heart, he soon became a ruling elder (church board/council member). The winter of Marty's second year, the session (church board/council) and I gathered on a retreat together, and we asked ourselves, *What is keeping us from noticing what God is doing and joining it without hesitation? What unspoken fears or beliefs are holding us back?*

We gave language to four big assumptions that, as a community and as individuals, we regularly, unwittingly rehearsed:

1. Our glory days are in the past.

2. We are too small, too old, and we don't have enough money.

3. If you volunteer for something, you'll be stuck for life.

4. A few people do all the work.

We wrote these big, fear-based assumptions on a large sheet of paper and looked at them for a few minutes. Every one of them seemed absolutely true. Saying them aloud was a relief, actually.

Then we did something challenging. I asked them, "What is the opposite of these statements?" Saying the opposite of these things aloud felt scary. It felt like pretending. But we did it anyway.

And by this exercise we came up with these four statements:

1. God is doing something here and now that incorporates the past and leads us into the future.

2. We are exactly the right size and makeup, and have the resources we need, for what God wants to do in and through us.

3. Every person participates from their particularities and passions.

4. We all share the ministry of church.

When I first arrived at Lake Nokomis to be their pastor, in the main gathering room in the very center of the church building, where people assemble for coffee after every service, the whole wall, from one end to the other, was filled with eight-by-ten-inch confirmation photos, dating back to 1959. The earliest photos were black and white and featured smiling, robed, and corsaged young people standing three rows deep next to a pastor.

As the photos progressed into the 1970s and took on sepia tones, the robes gave way to bell-bottom pants and turtleneck tops, and there were two rows of kids instead of three, so the photos were closer up, the faces more discernible. Through the 1980s the hairdos expanded and numbers shrank, until the photo of the final class, somewhere in the late

1990s—a full-color, close-up picture of three young women standing next to a pastor. Because the photos were mounted in frames designed to hold three pictures each, the final two spots inside the frame were empty.

At every coffee hour, every church meeting, every community dinner or neighborhood event, participants gazed upon this testament, the photographic evidence of their decline. It stood as a monument to the past, visited twice a year by the adult children of members who came back to church with their parents for Christmas and Easter.

After some conversation, we took the photos down and put them in a swinging display off to the side. Now two displays replace those old confirmation photos. On one part of the wall is a collection of crosses from around the country and the world. Whenever a member or friend of the congregation travels, we invite them to bring back a cross. A couple of the crosses were sent to us from people in other places who have visited us, or from congregations we've had a connection with. It reminds us how big and vast is the body of Christ, the church, in the world.

On the other half of the wall are the four statements from that day on the retreat, the opposite of our fears. They are framed and hung, with a fifth sign, identifying them as "Our Guiding Convictions." God *is* doing something here and now and always. We *do* have everything we need for what God wants to do. People *do* participate from their particularities and passions, and we *all* share the ministry of the church. These statements are an expression of our trust in God and our belonging to each other, a picture of our life together.

A couple of years ago someone who had been with us for just a few years said to me, "I love looking at those; they describe us so well!" What she didn't know is that when we first hung them there, we didn't yet really believe them. But we hung them up anyway. And before long what at first felt false came to absolutely describe us.

We return to these guiding convictions when we need to remember what we know to be true. They were our particular way of reorienting ourselves out of fear and back to trust, and now they are faithful reminders that this is God's church and that we are joyfully along for the ride.

I've come to believe that Jesus was talking about something specific, here and now, when he was describing the kingdom of God. Every time Jesus invited people into the kingdom, he was speaking of a reality that exists, that he lived in completely, and calling others to live in it as well. It is the "real reality," as Richard Rohr calls it, the world defined by trust and not by fear. But it's not easy to see and even harder to choose, because another layer on top obscures the real reality.

One morning, when my daughter, Maisy, was seven years old, she awoke to discover that her water bottle from her bedside table had tipped and spilled all over a school library book, soaking the cover and causing the pages to ripple. In terror, she realized she would have to confess this to Ms. Storms, the dreaded school librarian.

Ms. Storms was larger than life. She was most often seen stereotypically shushing a group of kids with her finger to her lips and a fierce frown, then yelling into the room at large that all those children were distracting the other children with their shockingly loud and disrespectful noise. This immediately produced complete silence, which lasted, on average, a full seven to fifteen seconds before a low, whispery murmur began to build in the room, leading eventually to another outburst by Ms. Storms. Enforcer of Silence, Queen of Her Domain, Protector of the Books—this is who Maisy would have to face that day. All morning leading up to school, she anguished, tried to find ways out of it, tried to reason her way past the fear, but it clung fiercely.

Just before it was time to leave for school, when she was still very upset, I went to the basement to retrieve my snow pants, because, naturally, I would need them walking to school this early November week in Minnesota, where winter had already made its grand debut and the wind chill hovered at a respectable -3 degrees Fahrenheit. While I was fetching my snow pants, I noticed an extra pair that Owen had outgrown the year before. When I reached the top of the stairs, Maisy mentioned, out of the blue, that her friend Wyatt had been missing recess this week because he didn't have any snow pants.

"Maisy!" I said. "I just saw that we have an extra pair that is probably his size!"

Her face lit up, and she said, "Oh, Mom! Let's bring them!"

So I went back and grabbed the snow pants. She found a bag to put them in and mused over how excited Wyatt would be to get them.

After a minute or two, she looked at me, a bit shocked, and said, "Mom! I don't feel scared right now!" And we marveled at how, when she moved momentarily from worry to generosity, from fretting to sharing, her fear lifted, and she felt alive.

Refocusing didn't take all the fear away, but I watched her walk to school, her eyes alight, as she deliberately chose to concentrate on Wyatt and the snow pants instead of on Ms. Storms and the library book. They were both waiting for her when she arrived at school. She was going to have to face both of them. But somehow, when the moment came to speak to Ms. Storms, instead of the tentative, terrified, and teary girl she had thought she would be, she was calm—nervous but clear-voiced. As she took my hand and walked steadily to the librarian's desk to face down her fear, she knew that she was more than a book-wrecker; she was a snow pants–sharer too.

Old Testament scholar Walter Brueggemann famously describes two competing scripts in the world, two narratives that unfold in Scripture and define how we live and move and have our being.[1] These two scripts are on display all around us and certainly throughout the biblical narrative. In what he calls "the dominant script," the powerful matter; the weak do not. This script says that having more makes you better; your worth is earned. Other people are nothing more than competition for resources or obstacles in your way; they should be used to further yourself, or eliminated. Life begins in self-sufficiency, and you'd better not screw up. Those who make mistakes or are no longer productive will be judged, labeled, and dismissed. There is not enough to go around, so you should take what you can get before someone else does. God is keeping score; you should be too. This perspective is also called "alienation" by David Steindl-Rast, and Thomas Merton calls it "the false self." In our congregation, we call it "the way of fear."

The other script, the "kingdom of God script," says that life begins in gift, and abundance. You are made by God for connection and communion. You are loved just as you are. You are not meant to be perfect (there's no such thing); you are meant to be *you*. On this journey of life that begins in gift and ends in connection and communion, the people journeying alongside you are neighbors, friends, and siblings—not threats, rivals, or competitors. You need each other to be whole, and what you have is for sharing. Life doesn't make sense when you are alone and isolated and against; you are created for relationship with God and with each other, and there's no such thing as a relationship with God without other people, or relationship with other people that doesn't involve God. This is what Rohr calls "the real reality," Steindl-Rast calls "interdependence," and Merton calls "the true self." Our congregation calls this script "the way of God."

The dominant script—the way of fear and alienation—shapes life around the avoidance of pain and the pursuit of personal gain. The false self is dominated by attitudes of control, mistrust, grasping, and scarcity. This is the lens that produced our first, unspoken fears that unwittingly guided our congregation. *We are not enough; there is not enough.*

The kingdom of God script—the way of God and interdependence—shapes life around the wisdom of Micah 6:8: everyone having what they need, *mishpat* (justice); standing with you/belongingness, *hesed* (kindness); and being attentive and open, *hatzn'a* (walking humbly with God). The true self is our deepest reality of being loved by God and connected to all others.

What does the Lord require? the verse asks. "Require," *darah*, is not like a test requirement or a harsh expectation. With undertones of affection, *darah* is like a child requiring her mother's love and flowers requiring sunshine—it's a *seeking*. It has a sense of interdependence. In the Old Testament, *darah* is used both for how lovers need, seek, and long for one another and for how a careful shepherd seeks a frightened lost sheep. What does the Lord require of us? Doing justice, loving kindness, and walking humbly with God. James C. Howell explains, "God seeks them, yearns for them, and frankly needs them from us as intimate partners in God's adventure down here."[2]

Doing justice (*mishpat*) is not about punishing evil and rewarding good; it is not about fairness. *Mishpat* means *ensuring that everyone has what they need. Do that* kind of justice—caring for the neediest among you; the expression is active, not passive. God is inviting all of us to be sharers, to build a deeper, richer kind of community.

Loving mercy and kindness (*hesed*) is our word with no English equivalent. *Hesed* is the belongingness we unpacked earlier, from the book of Ruth. This belongingness is "lovingkindness," compassion, with a fiercely loyal commitment to stand by each other no matter what. *Hesed*, belongingness, is the very fabric of our life together in the kingdom of God. *Standing-with-you.* And we are to *love* it—to wake up thinking about it and watch for it throughout the day. We are to revel in it, write songs about it, and let it invade us and shape us, this belongingness.

And finally, there is walking humbly with God (*hatzn'a*). This is a rare word in ancient Hebrew, so rare that scholars are not *completely* sure what it means. It could be translated as something like "attentively," "wisely," "carefully," or "with humility." It's to move about our lives in the simple truth about ourselves and God—being honest about who we are and who God is.

We will be tempted to import the words *justice* and *kindness* into the way of fear. We will want to judge ourselves by how well we're doing justice or loving kindness. We will feel like measuring others by their failure to do either one. We will compete, rank, try to score points with God or others, and even gauge how humble we might be at the moment. But this text reminds us that we're called to be honest and attentive, human alongside other humans, broken, struggling, and imperfect. We have a God who loves us with a *hesed* kind of love and who is calling us always and ever into a *mishpat*, *hesed*, *hatzn'a* kind of life in the world. And we are to focus on that God, instead of always measuring our own or others' worthiness.

Trusting in the abundance, guidance, and care of God is what gets lived out in our congregation's guiding convictions. In God, there is more than enough. Daily, we are given many, many chances to choose which way we will live, which message we will believe, and which reality will define us, the way of fear or the way of God.

The Bible is full of stories in which the people of God face this choice. One of them is found in Isaiah 36–37. Things are looking pretty grim for the people of God. They are faced with another chance to pick a script, to choose which way they will live and which message they will believe. The messages are trumpeted loudly by the General, the voice of alienation and fear, and the Prophet, the voice of interdependence and God. Will they listen to the General or the Prophet? The story goes like this:

Great Big, with its terrifying army, is right at the doorstep, and it has wiped out everything in its path—destroying cities and killing every inhabitant. Assyria is a force to be reckoned with. And little Jerusalem seems not to stand a chance. And now the Great Big Assyrian General is taunting, loudly and publicly, mocking Israel's King Hezekiah. The General is roaring, logically and convincingly, inviting all who hear to shift allegiance to the powerful side, because we all know how this is going to go down. And the idea that somehow "god" will save them is ludicrous! No other "gods" have done any saving of any other people this army has wiped out on their way here. "Say what you will," Great Big blusters, "but when it comes down to it, the power is ours, and we will destroy you either way."

But then Little Tiny is reminded by the Prophet Isaiah that God tells a different story about them. And it's not just that they will be, somehow, miraculously saved from obliteration. It's that, beyond saving them from destruction, God has a purpose for them. A really lovely, hopeful purpose, past what either side can see in the moment. The voice of the Prophet says God wants Little Tiny to bless the whole world! To take the very weapons of violence and make them into tools of life-giving community and sustenance for all (Isa 2:1–4).

And even though logic and might are on the side of Great Big, and even though it looks like Little Tiny will certainly be crushed, still, Little Tiny is invited to live defiantly into a different view of the future. They are invited to move from worry to generosity, from fretting to sharing. They are called to trust that God will sustain them and, even more, that God will use them to bring life and hope to the world.

The story of God asks us, again and again, *Which voice will you listen to? Which script will you live in?* You get this one, "wild and precious life," as poet Mary Oliver puts it.[3] How will you live it? As a congregation, we get this beautiful and daring shot at being a community of Jesus-followers together. How will we live it? If it's all gift, given by the generosity and grace of God, inviting us to join Jesus in sharing life with each other in love and hope—how will we play the hand we've been dealt? How will we spend the years, the days and hours, the resources and relationships that we have? What will our gifts be for? Who will we be?

Again and again, this little community I pastor chooses to live in trust instead of fear, to be guided by purpose instead of pressure, to recognize that this ministry is God's and not ours. But this only works if God is real and is leading us; it doesn't work if "God" is just a belief or an idea made of platitudes and doctrine. Because if God isn't real—if we say that God is real but in our hearts, God is just an idea and the Christian life is just about trying to do good things or be good people—then we should probably listen to the voice of the General, which says, "You're tiny. Can you even afford a pastor? You've been spending down your endowment forever; at the rate you've gone, you only have a couple of years left. The fact that you're still here is just luck. There is no future for you. Why don't you just give up? You're going down eventually anyway. The church at large is going down; just look at all the evidence of your irrelevance. You've been beaten, tiny ones; it's time to face the facts."

But the voice of the Prophet gently asserts that God says to us, "You are mine. I have a purpose for you. You are not just to exist or survive; you are a beacon of hope and a place of sanctuary. You are given to each other and to those around you to share each other's burdens and joys and to seek me together. I will provide for you. I always have and I always will."

And so, over and over again, we make the choice. Which voice will we trust? The powerful voice of might and logic? Or the one that says God uses the weak and the broken, calls the unexpected and the unimpressive, works through the less-than-perfect instead of the have-it-all-togethers, who-ever they may be?

My congregation is not perfect, Lord knows. We're a scrappy, do-it-yourself affair. We are a little disorderly and unprofessional, and from time to time we drop the ball. And we are small, with a lot of old people and a lot of kids, and the people in between are stretched thin, so we don't look like a convincing, get-it-done kind of crew. Let's just say a gambling person might not bet on us. The General certainly wouldn't advise it anyway.

But we are faithful and loyal and attentive and hopeful, and we have decades of standing-with-you belongingness under our belts. We know how to share each other's suffering. And we aren't afraid of doubt or differences. We are joyful and creative and full of life, and we long for life and joy in the communities and people around us. We are seeking, and we are hungry, and we are broken and we are blessed. And sometimes we forget and get scared. But when we trust God, we keep on finding ourselves blessing others and receiving blessings unforeseen.

If this life is about competition and power and requires self-sufficiency and the pursuit of perfection, then what my little congregation does is more than irrelevant; it's ridiculous. It's absurd to invest any time or money or belief or hope in such vulnerable people and such a homemade little operation. There are far stronger and more impressive things we could be involved in. We should listen to the General.

But if this life is about relationship with God and each other and it requires trust and dependence on God and a little bit of honesty and bravery, then perhaps the very *worst* position to be in is strong and self-sufficient. Maybe the very *farthest* we can get from grace is when we believe we have got it all together or when we're obsessed with the awareness that we haven't.

Fear is so powerful. It will define life as a battle and make us want to hunker and hide and hoard. But love is more powerful. And when the real reality breaks in, when the kingdom of God punctures through our layers of fear and self-protection, we see each other and ourselves as we are: beloved children of God, called to live in defiant resistance to the message of fear, in the joyful generosity and extravagant hope of our calling, not too proud to be something God can work with.

As the story goes, King Hezekiah, on getting another taunting threat letter from King Sennacherib, now calmed by the voice of the Prophet, is able to go into the sanctuary himself and approach God, and he prays, "God, you alone are God; you made all things. See what this King of Assyria is saying about you and is threatening to do to us? He's right; he did destroy all the gods of the other people they've conquered, but those 'gods' were just made of wood and stone and were not real. You are real. And you are God. And we are your people. Please save us."

And God does. We are told that the entire Assyrian army is "struck down in their sleep by an angel of God," and King Sennacherib, who headed home after receiving a message, is killed in his own town, worshipping in the house of his god, by his own sons. And even today, archaeologists and historians can't explain why Jerusalem was not destroyed in the Assyrian rampage that swept through the land.

And for a time, the people chose to live by the voice of the Prophet instead of the General. They were guided by trust instead of fear. They remembered that they belonged to God and that God had called them to a life of interdependence, to join in God's world-healing purpose beyond themselves and their own survival.

In the end, it turned out that Wyatt's new snow pants had come in the mail the day before, so Maisy donated the extra ones to the classroom for the next time someone needed them. And along with a lecture about the alarming capacity of mold to destroy entire libraries and advice on the proper care of books, Ms. Storms showed Maisy great empathy. "I bet you felt really bad, didn't you?" she asked her. Maisy nodded, her eyes brimming up. "Well," said Ms. Storms, "I know that you are a conscientious girl and that you love books too. Thank you for telling me what happened. Now I can take care of this book and maybe even save it."

And Maisy walked away whispering to me, "Mommy, that went way different than I thought it would!" And she hugged me and bounced off to class.

And I stood there in the elementary school library flooded with gratitude to God: for meeting us in these tiny, ordinary encounters that show us what is really real, in the moment when generosity reminded my girl that we are all connected, pulling her from the isolation of fear into the possibility of blessing; for meeting Maisy in the moment, allowing Ms. Storms to become a fellow human being working alongside her in this problem instead of a symbol of judgment and condemnation; and for meeting me in the chance to hold my daughter's hand through something hard and watch her be honest and brave.

By the time Marty got sick, we'd been talking about the way of fear and the way of God for a while. We'd even talked about the Prophet and the General and Maisy's tale of snow pants. We'd been watching for ways to live out our belonging to God and to each other and practicing stepping into them when they presented themselves. We were learning to stop regularly and let God meet us in Sabbath to shift us out of the way of fear and back into the way of God. We were emboldened by naming and facing our fears, and we were regularly asking the living God to direct us. We were growing in trust that God was calling us and so would also meet us in that calling and give us what we needed to fulfill it.

Marty had just had an ER-worthy scare and was living on borrowed time when my family and I left for our trip to Australia and New Zealand. I was going to be away from church for a month. I agonized about what would happen if Marty were to die—or even to go into hospice—while I was away. My fear about this kept me up at night. But when I confessed it to them, my people reminded me, "We know how to be the church, Kara. We've got this." They helped me remember, and trust, that all ministry is God's ministry and all followers of Christ are ministers. And Marty's spiritual care was never in my hands; he was not mine to look after. He was God's, and God could be trusted with him. So could the congregation. I realized it was good for me to go away, or else I might begin to see myself as indispensable in Marty's journey, instead of as a participant in God's ministry.

When we worry, we practice fear. When we rest, we practice trust. This is the essence of the Sabbath command: resting teaches us trust. So we notice when we start worrying and encourage each other to rest. I had started worrying. They reminded me to rest. I do the same for them when needed.

There are so many ways the way of fear is being exorcised from our midst, so many ways we rehearse living in the way of God. We practice presence. We say no like it's a complete sentence, and we say yes when we mean it. This has been a journey in and of itself—learning to say no to each other and even to ourselves. Last year the congregation voted *not* to hold its eighty-seventh annual Ham and Cherry Pie Dinner. For eighty-six years, this time-honored, iconic meal had been a defining feature of the congregation, and it had been faithfully attended for decades by neighbors and church alumni alike. The congregation's decision not to serve the cheesy potatoes, ham with raisin sauce, Swedish meatballs, rolls, green beans, sweet potatoes, and cherry pie was not made from a place of defeat. It was not a sign that LNPC was folding. They decided this because they realized that somewhere along the line—maybe even that very year—they'd begun doing it from obligation, for the purpose of upholding tradition, and not because it was bringing them joy and fulfillment. *It will be back*, they said, *for the one-hundredth anniversary of the congregation in a few years.* In the meantime, saying no to that tradition opened up an unexpected yes, when we realized we had energy for our first-ever, all-day, all-congregation "staycation." We spent a whole twelve-hour day together in the church building—all ages—doing crafts, playing games, worshipping, eating good food, resting, putting on a talent show, and playing. A deep-winter, daytime lock-in for all. The yes of this never would have happened if not for the no to the Ham and Cherry Pie Dinner.

We keep looking for ways to choose to live in the way of God instead of the way of fear. When we got scared about money, we started giving more of it away. When we got worried about our building, we started sharing it with more people, more groups, more congregations. When conflict arises, instead of moving away from it, seeking protection, we've started moving toward it, seeking connection. When our grip is tight and we feel like cowering and conserving, we pry open our own fingers and hold what we have before the Lord. We try to face and name our fears and then seek to live in the opposite way.

Always broader, always wider, always deeper, God's love is calling us, expanding us, bringing us *toward*. If we begin at rest, abundance, enough, joy, and trust, we can let whatever comes next flow from that. These are the things we are learning. We are eager, sometimes reluctant, stubborn, and sometimes fearful learners, but we mostly get there. And when we do, we find unfettered joy—freedom.

I didn't think I would be a pastor. My experience of church almost strangled my faith to extinction, and ministry seemed a dangerous weapon for the ego-starved to wield while hiding their own shame and weakness. And yet tending this precious space where souls come together with each other and with God is the most compelling thing I can imagine in life. So here I am, a pastor after all.

They didn't think they'd still be around. They'd had a good run, and dwindling numbers, falling finances, and aging members meant that other people gave up on them long ago. But they quit worrying about all that and turned to joy and gratitude instead, and here they are, a nimble, vibrant congregation after all.

Marty didn't think he'd be planning for an ending; he was preparing for a new beginning. But here he was anyway, living into his vulnerable humanity in a raw and real way. And we were alongside him. Together, we were *church*.

God was calling us to Marty, to be with and for him as he died, and to receive from him his Ministry of Dying. And because God doesn't waste anything, all of our experiences leading to this point were part of our story. The Holy Spirit integrated them into who we were alongside Marty and one another: the worship that remembers our belonging to God, the hospitality that practices our belonging to each other, and the Sabbath rest that helps us abide in this belonging that defines us.

Chapter 8

That We Might Have Joy

———

Who am I? They often tell me
I would step from my cell's confinement
calmly, cheerfully, firmly.
like a squire from his country-house.

Who am I? They often tell me
I would talk to my warders
freely and friendly and clearly,
as though it were mine to command.

Who am I? They also tell me
I would bear the days of misfortune
equally, smilingly, proudly,
like one accustomed to win.

Am I then really all that which other men tell of?
Or am I only what I know of myself?

restless and longing and sick, like a bird in a
    cage,
struggling for breath, as though hands were
    constricting my throat,
yearning for colors, for flowers, for the voices of
    birds,
thirsting for words of kindness, for neighborliness,
trembling with anger at despotisms and petty
    humiliation,
tossing in expectation of great events.
powerlessly trembling for friends at an infinite
    distance,
weary and empty at praying, at thinking, at
    making,
faint and ready to say farewell to it all?

Who am I? This or the other?
Am I one person today and tomorrow another?
Am I both at once? A hypocrite before others,
And before myself a contemptible woebegone
    weakling?
Or is something within me still like a beaten
    army,
fleeing in disorder from victory already achieved?

Who am I? They mock me, these lonely ques-
    tions of mine.
Whoever I am, Thou knowest, O God, I am thine.

—DIETRICH BONHOEFFER,
Letters and Papers from Prison
(written shortly before his
execution by the nazis)

W hen Marty's *Who am I?* shifted from "man on the brink of an exciting retirement" to "person dying of cancer," still, this was not what defined him. Such a thing—even a thing as big as this—doesn't have the power to determine our true identity.

According to Andrew Root's work on Charles Taylor's "secular age" theory, we live in a time when, more than ever before in history, it is presumed in Western culture that the purpose of life is to define your own identity for yourself.[1] *Who are you going to be?* the world relentlessly asks. Nobody else can tell us who we are; that's exclusively *our* job, it's our main job, and it's our highest job. Defining and curating our own identity has become such an important project in Western, modern culture that we do it all the time without even realizing we are doing it.

Defining and curating our own identity requires comparing ourselves to others nearly constantly. It means knowing what identities are available so we can figure out where we fit and listening to others who reflect our chosen identities so we know more how to be whatever they are, whatever we are, so that we can find community or ensure respect by fitting in well enough with whatever that identity happens to be.

The tricky part is, some aspects of our identity change—in fact, a lot of them do—because people change. We're defined by our current developmental state, as babies, children, teenagers, young adults, middle-aged, or elderly. We move from student to master, from amateur to professional to retired, from employed to unemployed, from ability to disability, health to sickness, and back again, perhaps several times. We grow into and out of our preferences, hobbies, even our goals. And over time, our beliefs change. The thing we previously held dear, that we might even have shaped our whole life around, no longer is central or becomes more nuanced, or we trade it out for something else entirely. And now something new defines us. This new thing becomes our identity—until something happens that might shift that again.

We move to a new place, we lose our spouse, our career ends, our health changes, our child comes out to us, we become our parent's caregiver, our church falls apart, new questions arise in our spirit, new callings emerge. And on and on, our identity keeps shifting.

Our identity isn't even consistent from one context to another. With one group of friends, we might be the outgoing one; with another group, the quiet one. In one situation we might be related to everyone in the room; in another, we might be the only woman, or the only Black person, or the only English-speaker. So even though we think our identity is ours alone to create and shape, it has something to do with those around us and the role we play in the group.

Then to complicate things, our culture puts pressure on us to be immediately identifiable in our self-chosen labels so that even though we're supposedly unique, others should be able to properly categorize and label us as a "type." People want to know, Are you a Republican or a Democrat? Are you progressive or conservative? An ally? An enemy? What do you do for a living? Where do you live? Do you rent or own? Are you single, or do you have a partner? Did you come from somewhere else, or are you from here? We won't admit it, but we want to be able to make assumptions and snap judgments about people based on things like education level, finances, or body weight. (According to a recent study, body weight is the one area today where stereotypes and prejudices are increasing, while in all other areas, such as race, religion, or sexual orientation, rates of prejudice are dropping.)[2]

And it really throws us for a loop when people don't fit neatly into our categories. What do we do with a Black, gay, Republican, Christian pastor with Asperger's, like my colleague Dennis?[3] Which table does he get assigned to in the lunchroom of life? I read that the Women's March founders—for all their unity of goals and perspective—had a personal rift because they differed on whether the Jewish member was part of the dominant white culture or a marginalized person. Was she a victim of oppression or part of the oppressive power structure? We can't imagine being more than one thing; our categories are exclusive and conclusive. We need to know what label to assign a person so we know how to treat each other.

We need to know if you belong, or who belongs more, or who needs to work harder to belong. In a time when our main job is to create and curate our own identity, we had better not slip up and mislabel others or ourselves, and we'd better not lose a prized label once it's secured. People are always paying attention. Everything we say and do is evidence of our belonging or not-belonging, and our place and potential in the world will be shaped by our self-defined identity and others' perceptions of it. So choose carefully and walk delicately.

This is a new thing. In the past, identities were pretty much given to people by their community. They didn't get a say, because it wouldn't have occurred to anyone that it was the individual person's job to figure that out. For better or worse, people simply were defined by where and to whom they were born—their status and role in society were predetermined. They just lived into it. Of course, this system had its own serious problems, but people were not swimming in options and drowning in expectations as they figured out their own slippery identity and tried to live it out in the world.

Jesus was the Messiah. This is a one-and-only role, never before lived into, with a collection of deeply held expectations at the get-go. Messiah was supposed to liberate the people from an oppressive empire, to bring in a revolution, restore the nation of Israel. The Messiah belongs to Israel. Messiah is strong, extraordinary, powerful, and obvious, not vulnerable or ordinary, weak or hidden. Here's what Messiah was. Who are you going to be, Jesus?

Jesus's whole life thwarted long-held "Messiah" expectations pretty radically from his first breath. Born in a stable, being honored by a bunch of pagan mystics from a far-off land for his cosmic significance to the whole world, spending the first few years of his life as a refugee, and then apparently living such an ordinary, small-town, Middle Eastern Jewish upbringing that it's not even worth mentioning, with an unremarkable appearance and nothing that set him apart as conspicuously Messiah-like. And he hadn't come to overthrow the Romans!? He came to overthrow death!? We don't have a category for that one. Before the Messiah's ministry even begins, Jesus is facing down all sorts of expectations and assumed identities, but there's only one identity that matters. And it's declared at his baptism.

John (the Baptist) has been preaching and raving in the wilderness, and people are flocking to be chastised by his strong language and powerful rhetoric and then to be baptized by him. And Jesus shows up there, just, it seems, as John references this Messiah that is coming, one who is so important that John would not be worthy of even untying his sandals and washing his feet like a servant. But Jesus slips into the crowd, according to Luke's telling (Luke 3:15–22), and gets baptized right alongside the rest of them. John seems not to pause in the act, and rather than stopping himself from washing the Messiah's feet, or acknowledging to him, as Peter will later, his unworthiness to wash the Messiah's feet, John proceeds, apparently, to wash him completely, just like he does the person before and the person after him. And then the Holy Spirit descends in bodily form like a dove, and Jesus hears the words spoken over him like a pronouncement: *You are my child, my beloved; I am delighted with you.*[4]

All the things Jesus was "supposed to" be and do, all the messages shaping even his own beliefs about Messiah, the people's intense expectations for a Messiah, the relentless *Who are you going to be?* put upon Jesus—they die here at his baptism. And what rises is only the connection with God, only his identity as beloved, only his purpose of embodying the love of God to us and us to God.

Baptism is an enactment of dying and rising. This gets missed with the gentle Presbyterian head sprinkle but is easier to see with the Baptist-style full-immersion dunk. We are baptized into Jesus's own death and resurrection. We acknowledge that we die. As Andy spoke over baby Owen ("Welcome to humanity. You will die"), we are, in fact, given over to death. And then we are raised up in Christ's life. Jesus's own relationship with God, his identity, becomes ours—permanently sealed into the love of God. Receiving God's Yes and saying yes back, living toward God as God lives toward us, is our purpose, acknowledged in baptism.

Right after his baptism, Jesus is sent by the Holy Spirit into the wilderness to face temptation—all the things that would try to claim and shape his identity. *Who are you going to be?* the tempter will ask him. *Will you be invincible? Will you use your power to escape pain and suffering and instead be given honor?* But when he comes up out of that water and hears spoken his true identity, he is already freed from these temptations. The temptations he hasn't yet faced in the wilderness, and those to come every day after that, are part of what he's prepared by his baptism to let go.

Baptism is not some kind of magical act. Ordinary water, ordinary words, ordinary people watching, pouring water, and making promises. But in this ordinary moment, we trust that God—who always has claimed us for love—now becomes the source of our identity. The love of God becomes our purpose. The grace of God becomes our belonging. Baptism is the convergences of yeses, God's and ours, back and forth.

All other identities—whether long-term or temporary, inherent or chosen, released or reclaimed, denied or explored, embraced or rejected—are not the identities that define us.

None of them is powerful enough or expansive enough to determine our deepest self and our truest purpose. There is but one identity that defines us first, last, and most completely. It is true of each of us before we came into being, and it remains true after we are gone from this earth: *Beloved. Child of God, in whom God delights.*

A photo hangs on Owen's bedroom wall. It is framed, with a date on the bottom, March 6, 2005. In the picture, a short, stout, cheerful South African woman in a white alb holds in the crook of one arm a chubby, six-month-old, mostly bald baby boy dressed in white. His perfectly round head is front and center in the photo, and his face is hidden from view. She is saying something, and the hand not holding him is cupped above him, water dripping down from the backs of her fingers. Owen's baptism. We placed the picture directly across from his bed when he was three years old.

Owen struggled for a while, when he was very young, with terrible nightmares. They were frightening visions that made him feel unsafe, alone, terrified to be in his room at night. We tried to comfort him in various ways, praying for him, cuddling him, leaving the door open and the hall light on. We told him that Jesus was with him, and this just frustrated him. "I can't see Jesus!"

We told him angels were there and that just freaked him out. "I don't want *them* in here!"

Finally, we told him the story of his baptism. "You belong to God," we said. "You've been baptized. Jesus's love is stronger than death; it broke death forever, and you belong to this love. When you feel afraid, when things seem big or scary, look at this picture. This is your baptism. Do you know what this means?" we asked. And then he first heard the mantra that became our children's comfort in fear: "Death can't get me, because Jesus has got me."[5]

When life knocks him down and breaks his heart in two, that picture on his bedroom wall is testimony that no matter what others say about him, no matter how deeply he doubts his worth, no matter how lost he feels in trying to determine who he is and what his life is for, and no matter how hard he denies it or how loudly he may shout *no* to his most intrinsic identity and belonging, God has already said *Yes*. It is irreversible and permanent. He belongs to God.

Despite the relentless messages around us, our primary job is not, in fact, to construct our own identity in the world. That has already been decided for us. Our first job, our only job, is to live into the identity decided for us before the foundation of the world. We are made in God's own image to share this life with God. The grace of God reaches out to us by the Holy Spirit, and brings us back, every time we forget—and we forget many times a day. But God's grace always brings us back to our truest, deepest identity: *Beloved. Child of God, in whom God delights.*

A few months after we told Owen the story of his baptism, our three-year-old son looked on curiously from his dad's hip as a pastor poured water and spoke words of belonging over his wailing baby sister, Maisy. He heard her identity declared by the pastor and echoed by the people—*Beloved! Child of God!*—settled and irreversible. What he was watching matched the photo on his bedroom wall! What he was hearing was just like what had happened to him!

Life is a gift to be lived in response to God's grace. Each one of us is completely unique, unequaled in all the world, all of us beloved children of God. Each one of us is a mix of contradictions and conundrums, beauty and ugliness, struggle and gladness, a glorious hodgepodge of features and facets. Not one of us fits easily into human categories or labels, nor should we. We are each meant to be the one and only you or me that has ever walked, or will ever walk, on this earth.

We can trust that our identity isn't up for grabs. It is secure. Unshakable and permanent. It cannot be altered or abolished. It cannot be lost, and it cannot be earned. It isn't some nugget of unchanging self we hold within and cling to. And it isn't a shiny new object we choose for ourselves from the world's endless array of enticing options. Our identity is bestowed upon us by the Creator of all, given to us by the one who comes in alongside us. We are who we are because God sees and knows the whole of us and loves us completely. God holds the continuity of all we have been and all we will be in a single, timeless gaze of love.[6] And in baptism, this identity is recognized, confirmed, celebrated, witnessed, and sealed.

In baptism, death gets spoken over us first. *You will die.* This is good news—first because it's true, and baptism tells the truth, but also because in baptism we die to any identities we, or those around us, thought made us who we are, and we die to all identities we may one day feel drawn, or pressured, to take on. They no longer have the power to determine our being or define our ultimate worth. As useful as these labels or definitions may be in guiding us at points in our lives, or helping us reclaim or respect parts of ourselves, they cannot give us our deepest purpose or take away our fundamental belonging. We don't need to fear death or avoid it—even if we're threatened with loss, rejection, or obliteration. Jesus died for us. Jesus's death takes on our death and we take on his.

And then resurrection. We rise to a new life, a new identity in Christ, with Christ: *Beloved. Child of God, in whom God delights.* Belonging forever to God. This identity will never fade. This purpose will never disappear. This belonging will never end.

Marty was baptized as a baby in a Presbyterian church. These words were spoken over him before he could grasp them or hope to remember them. Marty spent a lot of his life chasing his own *Who am I?* and the world's *Who are you going to be?* But the truth of his identity had already been decided and spoken over him before any of that work had even begun. And now he was leaning back into his essential identity, because all the other identities he had claimed or formed for himself, all the things bestowed on him by others or assumed about him by the world, had fallen by the wayside.

The new identities now being offered to him—patient, dying person—were temporary and imposed. They did not have the power to determine who he was. The only one who can really tell us who we are is God. And God names us *Beloved.* This is our true self. Marty was rediscovering that it is not our job to define or uphold our identity, only to live into the identity decided for us already by God. And to live it boldly.

As his death loomed, Marty lived in a kind of boldness. A few months in he said to me in a joyful kind of chagrin, "Kara,

I know I am supposed to be showing people how to die, but I feel like I am showing people how to live." And he was. There was a joyful fearlessness to him in those days.

Interspersed between medical appointments and his increasing need for rest, Marty spent his days in surprising joy, meeting with friends for lunch, walking around the lake, reconnecting with people from his past, having spontaneous get-togethers, appreciating the little things, awake to the gift of it all.

In the way of fear, there is no time to stop or rest or let up, even for a moment, or you will get behind, lose your place. When life is shaped around the avoidance of pain and pursuit of personal gain, when you are constantly building and upholding your own identity, when the goal is security at all cost, and when the world is most often dangerous and urgent, joy doesn't make sense. Being joyous can seem almost like a violation. If you have too much gladness, you must not be paying attention.

There are so many pressing demands. There is so much to be worried or angry about. So much suffering and injustice, we could spend all day, every day dwelling only on that. So perhaps in today's way of life we see joy as gaudy, naive, or thoughtless. Perhaps we think it's more polite, or woke, to hide our joy, or temper it with caveats, so it doesn't make others feel bad. We treat joy like a weapon that can wound those who are already suffering, or like a limited commodity—there is only so much to go around, and if one person has too much joy, they are hogging it from others and should feel guilty.

But what if you are the suffering one *and* the joyful one? What if anger and worry no longer work for you? Perhaps when all of that falls away, when you've already "lost" the game—your life is ending, you're out of the race, the death you've spent your life denying and avoiding is coming for you after all, and there is nothing you can do about it—you're also closer to the truth of existence, more able to be fully alive.

Joy is the feeling of being fully alive. When we are completely at home in our true identity—even momentarily—what we feel is joy. We are singing our "heart song" when we feel the energy of being connected to God and knowing who we are, and whose. And heart song it isn't just one high, cheerful note; it's the whole tune, with all its complexity. The low, groaning, moaning parts from the depths of our lonesome souls, the laughter-tinged merriment of high notes, the goosebumpy harmonies and steady favorite melodies, and the rhythm that keeps the beat of it all. It's the fully singing heart with all its parts. Joy is not an adversary of suffering; it's a friend and collaborator. God's grace meets us in suffering, and grace brings joy when we find ourselves receiving our lives as a precious and beautiful gift.

Jesus said all he said and did all he did so that we might have his joy—joy that comes from being fully alive, fully connected to the Father, fully at home in love (John 15), fully at rest in our identity as Beloved, Child of God. God's intention for us is to bring us back in alignment with God and with our true self that already knows God. God's joy spilled out and gave life and breath to a universe; this is what God wants to sync us up to. When we feel in sync with the universe, we feel joy.

Joy feels absurd and wonderful, disrupting the ordinary and suddenly overwhelming us with delight. Joy is our recognizing an inconceivable glimpse of the innate and inde-structible depth of our true identity. This is why flash mobs make me cry. And surprise reunions. Joy shows us our under-lying belonging to each other. Once, when I was a kid, my little sister's boisterous laugh ignited a whole movie theater. We missed an entire scene of the movie because the whole room was laughing at ourselves laughing. Buoyant, ridiculous joy grounds us in truth—that there is something beyond and beneath us, holding us all together. Joy shatters the false with real, tangible experiences, transcendence that comes upon us only when we're right here, fully present. Joy backs fear into a corner with its overwhelming, unabashed celebration of life and living.

Marty was a living and dying testimony to this. When we exist in grace, and we're no longer concerned with saving our life, or earning or proving anything, we're open to joy. When we feel the depth of being loved, when we love others from our depths, when we receive God's presence as love and our own life as a gift—not earned, not deserved, not only for the "worthy," but meant for *us*, this life, all its beauty and all its pain, unique and unequaled anywhere else on the planet, our one gift of a heart-singing life held in love—we taste joy. When we accept that our only identity is Beloved, Child of God, we are suddenly, frequently, overcome by joy. This is what Marty was showing us.

One day the whole damn system will be overthrown. All fear and competition and striving and judging and rushing and destruction and death of every kind will end. Mary sang out this prophecy in the Magnificat (Luke 1:46–55), when the fetus John leaped for joy in Elizabeth's womb, recognizing the Messiah that Mary carried within her. *The day is coming,* she sang out, *when the poor and lowly will be lifted up and the strong will be made weak.* [What we believe makes us strong is all a farce anyway.] *All wrongs will be made right; only life—the full love and belonging of God—will remain.*

One day all time itself will be different—measured by delight instead of deadlines, counted out in laughter and tears instead of accumulated accomplishments. One day all alienation will utterly crumble away, leaving only love. Joy remembers this future that is to come; it "premembers." Joy summons us awake. It gives us strength to stand in the confusion and loss and embrace the deeper truth of our belonging to God and each other because joy premembers our deepest belonging.

While certainly he didn't always stay there, Marty was living in the present, ever more open to the interconnected way of God. He was singing his heart song. He was embracing his true identity: Marty the Beloved, Child of God, in whom God delights. His living this way near us drew us in and invited us to do the same. Joy is nothing if not contagious.

Chapter 9

When We Face Death

But if we have died with Christ,
we believe that we will also live with him.
We know that Christ,
being raised from the dead,
will never die again;
death no longer has dominion over him.
The death he died, he died to sin,
once for all;
but the life he lives,
he lives to God.

> —THE APOSTLE PAUL (ROMANS 6:8–10;
> formatting mine)

We're all just walking each other home.

> —RAM DASS, from Ram Dass and
> Mirabai Bush, *Walking Each Other Home*

*E*ven though he didn't come across as a particularly out-spoken trailblazer or an overly strong personality, Marty had often paved the way without meaning to or knowing he was doing so. Not until I look back do I recognize what a leader Marty was among us.

He was the first to take the new-member vow to let us be church with and for him, to share his suffering and joy, and he fulfilled that vow consummately. Alongside the other elders, he helped us move from fear to faith in coming up with those guiding principles of trust.

A few years into his time at the church, when Marty became treasurer, we began slipping back into fear as we watched our savings dwindle. The session, seeking a practice to help us remember that this is God's church and not ours and that God (not money) is our security, voted then to begin tithing. We would give away 10 percent of all we brought in to some other expression of God's ministry in the world. We are, after all, only one small part of the vast body of Christ. As trea-surer, Marty had a front-row seat on the finances, watching how what we were giving away widened our belonging. Our gifts connected us to others and even came back to us unex-pectedly, as when Pastor Antonio pulled up to the front of our building and told us the Holy Spirit had directed him to ask if his congregation might meet in our basement. So we wel-comed in a new community whose donations almost exactly matched what we were giving away each month.

When our Sabbath practice began teaching us that trust-ing God with our church meant each of us serving only out of joy and not out of obligation, we wrote that right into the elder vows from that point forward. *Will you serve from joy and only as long as it gives you joy?* we'd ask new elders. And every year we began asking the congregation, among other end-of-year reflection questions, *What would you like to keep doing? What would you like to stop doing?* Marty was the first to stand up in a congregational meeting and gratefully step out of a role, as treasurer, before the joy had completely left him and obligation was all that remained. We got to celebrate and thank him and release him from his duties without pressure. He opened the door for others to do the same after him.

And then, of course, he was blazing the way by dying so openly in front of us.

Marty lived these days in a suspended Sabbath time. He no longer measured his life by what he accomplished; he no longer measured it at all. He no longer compared or competed or focused his life on doing. Instead, he lived in his being. He simply was. He received each day as a gift, as awake to the presence of God and of others as he could be. He was poignantly aware of what an astonishing thing it is to be alive. Marty had stopped—all the striving and climbing and saving his own life. His life was already lost. And so, in the freedom of that, he rested. He rested in the love of friends and the love of God. He was held in grace. He belonged to us and to God; we belonged to him and to God. Our sharing his suffering together held all of us in an experience of profound grace. We could not see a way through this that avoided pain; we could only share his pain and ours, and there encounter Christ.

This is not to say he was immune to terror or sorrow. Several times a sudden hospital stay, a further diagnosis, or a new symptom plunged Marty into fear and despair. A friend gave him a trip to London, and at the last moment, he was forced to cancel. He was devastated. We met, and I prayed for him again.

The pain increased; the fatigue was sometimes paralyzing. He would sleep away a day without meaning to. When he felt like keeping from the rest of us the knowledge of how hard this all was, I would remind him of his vow to tell the truth to us. "You're false advertising if you make it look easy, Marty." And he would work up the courage to answer honestly about the pain, or the fear, whenever someone asked, "How are you?"

In early fall we set up a "care team" for Marty. The group's responsibilities included organizing a network for providing rides to the emergency room, night or day, and accompanying Marty to regular appointments. We met with his sister, Susan, his only family besides a previously distant brother with whom he was just beginning to reconnect. We would call Susan and offer support and a listening ear, or we would volunteer to take some responsibilities off her plate when they came to feel like too much. People queued up to pay for housecleaning, each donor covering a cleaning every two weeks. They were prepaid months in advance.

We urged Marty to spoil himself and to consider asking us for help when he felt any companionship needs—whether bored or lonely. We'd be ready to do whatever he wanted to do, we told him. Walks, movies, road trips, name it and we'd be there. *This is a gift to us*, we said.

We had meal prep on standby, organized by one person but joined by many. Meals progressed from occasional drop-in surprises to regular repasts when needed. Marty's apartment was up two flights of stairs, and eventually a system was devised whereby he'd drop the key out his apartment window to the person waiting below, who would bring the meal up rather than his having to come down the stairs to meet us.

When the question came up about how he would know when it was time to go into hospice, he really struggled with it. He didn't know how he would know. But we listened to him and heard him say, *When I can no longer leave my house*—that was a big marker for him. Independence and the ability to get out and do things was what made life worth living for Marty. It gave him joy. When there was no more joy left to living—no more ability to participate in the give and take of living, out there in the world alongside others—he would know he was nearing the end, so that became his sign, how he would know it was time. And we would remind him if he needed us to.

We took notes on all of these things and gave them to Marty and to his sister, Susan. Marty was very concerned that the cancer might affect his brain and very concerned that if it didn't, Susan still might think it did. Meeting with them regularly as a care team brought other ears, other voices, and reassurance into the picture, for both of them. All throughout, though the cancer never stopped spreading, Marty remained sharp. He was very grateful for that.

Marty and I met every couple of weeks. These meetings were precious, holy. His emotion was transparent. He was living more vulnerably than I had ever seen anyone live. I bore witness to his humanity, watching all the feelings cross his face as he spoke, holding his hand, laughing with him, and crying alongside him. He let the emotions come and didn't hold back. He was not captive to them, nor did he avoid them. They passed through him; he felt them, and then they dissipated and made room for the next emotion. It was astonishing to watch. In those times I bore witness to grace.

During these conversations, Marty would often circle back to two questions. The first was how many people the sanctuary could hold. "I have a lot of friends, you know." I would reassure him that we could accommodate everyone. It was so important to him that all those he loved would feel welcomed at his funeral. And second, he would return to a request he had made when he first realized cancer was going to take him. He wanted us to do for him something we had done years before for someone else—a woman named JoAnne (or Jo, as she was often called)—when Marty was a new member. "I'll let you know when I am ready," he would say.

"When you are ready, we will do it," I would answer.

"You guys, JoAnne is dying."

I watched tears spring to people's eyes and their faces crumple. I was moderating a session meeting, and the church's ruling elders were sitting around a table preparing to discuss the business of the church. Then I said aloud what we all knew to be true but nobody had acknowledged, maybe not even to themselves.

Jo is dying.

For six months people had taken turns driving her to chemotherapy appointments, as we'd all watched her grow weaker and frailer. In her late seventies, she had been the picture of health; now she was skin and bones. And she had stopped the appointments.

I had been pastor of the congregation for two years at that point. And one of the joys in the job was Jo. Jo was a spark of delight. Her spunk and humor were infectious. Not a formal leader in any sense, she still set the tone for how things went among her peers, pitched in wherever she could, and was adored by the whole congregation.

Jo had a special blend of honesty and mirth. My second Sunday as the church's pastor, I tried something out of the ordinary: I asked the congregation to break into groups and discuss a couple of questions I had projected on the screen. It did not go well. I was feeling shaky and embarrassed as I stood at the door and greeted people exiting the service. Jo bounced over to me. She grasped my hands, and with eyes alight and smile broad, she quipped cheerfully, "Well, that was just awful, wasn't it?" Somehow, instead of spiraling me into humiliation, it took the pressure off, and I laughed with her.

"Yes, it didn't go how I'd hoped," I answered.

"There's always next week!" she replied, grinning and patting my shoulder.

But now Jo was fading. It was soon obvious to me that we needed to do *something* and not just pretend Jo wasn't dying when we could all see clearly that she was. Two things had happened that had made that clear. The first had occurred when she returned from a family reunion a few weeks before. When I asked her how it was, she told me that she had taken along a T-shirt and fabric markers and had asked her whole extended family to sign her shirt. *She's creating her own liturgy!* I thought. The second had happened just the week before our session meeting. I had preached a sermon that ended with these words:

> We can't do anything about death, which comes for us all. And with the very biggest barns and most clever safety measures (Luke 12:13–31), we cannot prevent suffering or protect ourselves from pain or loss. But, nevertheless, we do not need to worry. Nevertheless, we are invited to live generously, freely, joyfully, rich toward God; we are invited to live without fear. Because our life is a gift from God, God's own treasure. It's not up to us to protect ourselves, preserve ourselves, or determine ourselves. We belong to God. God who made us and loves us and will not let us go. God who came and suffered death right alongside us, for us, so that we are not alone and so that death would not get the last word after all.
>
> Our treasure, our legacy, our true wealth, is our life, secure and made alive in Christ. Our life is a gift of love meant to be used and shared, meant to be lived fully and fearlessly in this passing world and one day forever in joy when God's kingdom is all in all. Amen!

When that service had ended, and I had gone to the back of the sanctuary to greet people at the door as they left, I had watched Jo struggle to stand and make her way very slowly with her walker to the rear doors. When she reached me, she hugged me. Then she kissed me on the cheek, pressed her own soft cheek against mine, and whispered into my ear, "I'm on my way." Pulling back and looking right into my eyes, she patted my arm and then slowly left the sanctuary.

This sent me into a series of sleepless nights. Jo knew she was dying; she was even creating her own liturgy around her death, and the church was pretending it wasn't happening. Why? Were we afraid that talking to her about it would alert her to her own ending? She already knew! She was accepting it. Was she afraid that talking to us about it would alert us to her own ending? We already knew! We could see it happening.

So *why*, I asked the session that evening, *are we not acknowledging this?* Why are we just going to let it happen and then talk about her after she's gone, but not do any kind of ritual for her, when rituals are what the church does? We mark baptisms, marriages, and confirmation. We have practices that recognize and honor milestones in people's life journeys. Why not the big one? *Why not dying?*

So we began hatching a plan. Our music director at the time, Jeanne, had worked as a hospice musician, playing her harp at people's bedsides. She was comfortable accompanying people through dying and talking openly with them about death. Together, she and I approached Jo. We knew if Jo was game for the sort of thing we were proposing, it would open the door for others to find their own way too. Jo was a trendsetter in the best sense of the word.

Jeanne and I went to Jo's house. I brought peach pie, and we sat at her table and told her what we were thinking. "Could we do a service for you?" we asked. "A 'keeping the faith' service—a way to recognize our love for you and your impact on us, a way to acknowledge your life before you are dead?"

At first she hesitated. Would it mean we had wrapped things up? she wondered. Would it be awkward to come back to church afterward, still alive? We assured her this wasn't a "goodbye," and we read together Paul's words in 2 Timothy 4:7: "I have finished the race, I have kept the faith." We told her we wanted to celebrate her life. We'd like to sing her favorite hymn and let people tell stories to her. She agreed.

When the day came, we placed an overstuffed chair in the center of the sanctuary. Our pews are set up in the round, so just behind Jo's seat was the baptismal font and faced the communion table, the symbols of our belonging to God; alongside her, and to the left and right of her, pews faced the center—a circle completed, a visual depiction of our belonging to each other. We put boxes of tissues in each row and predicted we'd be too much of a mess to share any kind of coffee hour afterward. We'd probably all just want to go home.

A quartet prepared Jo's favorite hymn, and I had put out the word: bring an object that reminds you of Jo, to tell a story about her. We placed by the door a basket for notes, for those who didn't want to share aloud. We were ready.

The day came, and I put on my clerical collar, my "funeral shirt." We settled Jo into the soft chair, a homemade quilt tucked around her, her hands resting in her lap and her smiling, impish face glancing around the room. As people filed in, the basket began to fill up with notes. Some had mailed their notes or sent them in with others instead of attending. Saying their words to her in person felt like too much.

I welcomed everyone and acknowledged that we were here because Jo's life was coming to an end. We were here to celebrate that she had "fought the good fight, finished the race, kept the faith." Here was our chance to tell her the ways her keeping the faith had impacted us. We would bring up our object, share a story, and place the object on the communion table.

I began with something light to break the ice and let people know this didn't have to be heavy. I pulled on a pair of bright-red gloves, with fuzzy rings around the wrists, that Jo had sewn for me. Raising them up to show them off, I said, "These remind me of Jo because she always wears gloves when she's handing out bulletins because her hands get cold." I took them off and laid them on the table. "Who would like to go next?" I asked, returning to my seat.

The next person was Butch. I had not known Butch to be a particularly emotive person; he was funny and smart and filled with trivia knowledge. Butch stood from his seat and came forward. He knelt at Jo's feet, and his eyes filled up. He took her hands in his. "I love you, Jo. There are no words to express what you mean to me and how much you have impacted me," he said to her. The tears began to flow.

Person after person brought forward items and told stories. The communion table began to fill up—jars of jam, recipe cards, Sunday school workbooks she had used to teach them when they were young. This is the table where we gather to be fed by God, the place we recount the brokenness of Christ's own body, where we come with our own vulnerability to be drawn into the real reality—our belonging to God and all those in the body of Christ who've gone before and who are yet to come. And we experienced that same communion together now, in the face of death.

The stories poured out. One person had set up a reel-to-reel projector and flipped it on to reveal Jo in her forties, dancing at a picnic with a wide sombrero on her head. Jo sat there soaking it all in, sometimes tearing up, most of the time grinning with delight.

We presented her with the basket of messages. The quartet sang. I knelt by her and anointed her—pointing out that she sat surrounded by her community, a cloud of witnesses, between the font and the table, the symbols of her faith. We spoke over her, "Well done, good and faithful servant" (Matt 25:23), and as the oil brushed her forehead, I proclaimed that she belonged to God and that her baptism would soon be complete.

And then it was over. But nobody wanted to leave. People stayed with Jo, talking, hugging, laughing, reminiscing, lingering with each other. Pretty soon someone went down to the kitchen and made coffee. Someone else filled a pitcher with cider and a plate with cookies, and these things were set on the communion table too. For two hours people lingered in that sacred circle together.

The following week I went to see Jo. She was in bed, the basket of notes next to her. She thanked me for the service and told me that she was showing the notes to everyone who visited and telling them what her church had done for her. She asked me to use that same Scripture at her funeral; she wanted me to proclaim after her death that she had fought the good fight, run the race, kept the faith. I told her I would.

Most of us don't get to see in our own lifetime how our lives have impacted others. We may have glimpses now and then, people may share with us their gratitude and love, but for the most part, we don't get to appreciate how we've made a difference in the world. Not so with Jo. We got to tell her. We got to thank her. We were brave enough to do this for her, because she was brave enough to let us.

Two weeks after that, Jo died. Her funeral was a celebration in the best sense of the word. We had already said all we wanted to, right to Jo herself. Now we got to tell those who were not there what that had been like. We had been prepared for this—this act of handing her over to God, letting her go from our midst. As funerals go, this one was easy. It felt joy-filled, the grief and loss no less real but somehow redeemed because they had been so deliberately shared.

Helping Jo go in that way, released by those who loved her, made her death and her funeral doorways for us all into the deepest belonging. There was no hiding, no unfinished business, no wishing for a chance to say one last word, no skirting the issue. This is what Marty was asking for. "What I loved about Jo's service was how everyone shared about their experiences with her. I want that too."

When I worked as a chaplain in a New Jersey hospital, I was in my midtwenties and pretty much terrified of death. I was assigned to the cardiac unit, where death sometimes happened, and the orthopedic surgery unit, where people often cried out that they wished death could happen because knee replacements are so much more painful than people are prepared for. I worked one on-call overnight shift a week covering the whole hospital, responsible for responding to Code 40s (when a team of forty people responds), Code Blues (when someone stops breathing), and situations in the emergency room (ER). On this assignment, death was more common.

I often revisit my time there in my mind. I see moments when I know I participated in what God was doing, and I feel grateful to have been there. But I also remember moments I am horrified by and have to release to God, trusting that God was not thwarted by my insecurity or missteps. It is sometimes painful to look back at life, wishing that I could bring my now-self to situations where my then-self seemed less than adequate to the task. Instead, I am invited to look at my then-self with compassion and to marvel at how much I have grown. (This too is grace!) Two encounters in particular stand out.

In one instance, when I was on call, I was paged by a doctor on the oncology floor. He had a patient who had received bad news. Her cancer had spread and was most certainly life-threatening, and he wondered if I could go and speak to her. I was frightened of the oncology floor. Heart disease felt predictable. Really old people whose hearts had given out, stressed-out middle-aged men with unhealthy eating and exercise habits, and young women caught up in the Atkins diet craze—that was my constituency. That felt manageable, foreseeable. Heart disease was a tornado with warning sirens and a trackable forecast, compared to cancer's earthquake or tsunami that came without warning, indiscriminately attacking anyone.

I'd been married a few years, and we were trying to conceive. We were both building our careers. Andy was doing his PhD program, and we were still living in student housing, longing to finish this stage and begin the next, with our whole futures stretched out before us. I needed for death to feel really, really far away.

I responded to the call and walked into a brightly lit room where a woman with her head wrapped in a colorful scarf was sitting on the bed. She seemed not much older than I was. Her mom was sitting facing her in a chair. They were leaning in and talking quietly with each other. Her mother seemed not much older than my own mother.

I took a deep breath and introduced myself. "Hi! I'm Chaplain Kara. Dr. Nelson told me you received some difficult news and asked if I'd stop in to see you."

It was then that I noticed the woman's three-year-old son, sitting on the floor, surrounded by crayons, and leaning into a coloring book. It nearly knocked the wind out of me.

I can barely remember what I said. The scene filled me with so much fear. I think I just kept repeating how lucky they were to have each other as support through this. Certainly I was no support. They were *not* lucky to have drawn the me-as-chaplain straw. I said a few inane things and got out of there before I hyperventilated. I passed on the call to the chaplain of the oncology unit, a sturdy nun in her sixties, to check in with the patient when she arrived. Then I went to hide in the bathroom in shame and confusion over the enormity of my terror.

The second incident was an encounter on my own cardiac unit with a woman in her nineties. When I entered her room, the blinds were open, the bright sun falling across the bottom of her bed. She was tucked in bed and sitting up, leafing through a newspaper. She glanced up when I entered, and her face broke into a welcoming smile. "Come in! Come in!"

"Hi, I'm the chaplain. I just came to visit with you and see if there is anything I can do for you."

"How old are you, my dear?" This was immediately embarrassing for me, because I looked much younger than my twenty-seven years, and I was asked this question a lot. My chronic longing to be taken seriously and not seen as "young" had stretched through most of my life, from kindergarten to that moment.

As I engaged her in conversation about her illness, she kept reframing things for me. I would say things that sounded hopeful, I thought, about her treatment or the doctor's skill, and she would tell me I was looking at it from my viewpoint. Finally, she interjected, "I'm old. I'm ready to die, my dear. You're just starting to live. You can't understand how it is for me, maybe. I'm not afraid. I have lived a good life. If this takes me, that will be OK." She patted my hand and returned to her paper. It was clear she was finished with my services, such as they were. Startled and humbled by her words, I left feeling useless and confused.

As a chaplain, I made it through several deaths, even a funeral, but most of my time in the hospital I teetered between truly holy moments and lots of inexplicable crying in the bathroom stall, trying to pull myself together to make cold calls, offering my spiritual services to my two hundred beds, or to sit with someone who was suffering. Finally, my supervisor told me I needed to be finished, and I was gently fired. "I'll give you two weeks, but you need to get out of here. This is clearly not good for you."

A fellow chaplain, Karen, the one with the worst unit of all, I thought, the children's hospital, stepped in. She caught me in the hall, in tears, reeling with relief and mounting panic. *What was I going to do next?*

"How much money do you need to walk away today?" Karen asked me. And then, right there in the hallway, she pulled her checkbook out of her purse and wrote me a check. She told me I could pay her back by cooking for her, three meals a week, and leaving them in her fridge to put in the oven when she got home. Chaplain Karen had two young sons, and her husband had died in a car accident two years before. She had a big fancy kitchen with new appliances that she never used because she couldn't bear to eat there without him. She couldn't bear to cook a meal for just her and her boys. They ate out most nights. Now she was asking me, when I was feeling weak and incompetent, to minister to her. She was giving me a calling.

My life shifted suddenly. Instead of going into the hospital, each week I emailed Karen a grocery list. Then on Monday mornings, instead of riding the train to life-and-death intensity, I drove over to her house, and in the still silence of her soaring ceilings and granite countertops, I looked out over her lovely backyard and chopped, mixed, and sautéed, pouring love into preparing food for Karen and her sons. When I finished washing the pots and pans, I wrote little notes for the top of each meal, and then I carefully arranged them on the refrigerator shelves.

I would picture Karen coming in, after picking her boys up from school in the giant SUV she'd bought after her husband's accident—added protection for her small sons. She'd toss her keys on the counter and preheat the oven, and soon the smells of lasagna or meat loaf would fill the house. Then she'd call her boys and they'd sit down together at the table.

When it was all ready, I wiped down the counters, turned off the light, and let myself out and went home. The next week I repeated the cycle. It was sheer grace. After two months, I had paid off my debt, and Karen had made peace with her dining table and begun to gently adopt new routines. It was grace for her too.

Before that, though, my last shift at the hospital was an overnight on-call. In the deep sleep hours of early morning, I was awakened by a Code 40. I always felt shocked when the pager woke me up, restlessly dozing in the tiny on-call room, to an emergency, and it took some deep breathing to get me into the right headspace to respond. I sat up for a moment in the darkness until I had composed myself. Then I sprang out of bed and pulled on my blazer, shoes, and badge and raced to the emergency room.

The patient was drunk, loud, HIV positive, and bleeding profusely from a gruesome leg wound, with a large, menacing knife sticking straight out of his thigh. Thirty-nine other people were converging on the scene. Everyone was pulling on plastic protective garments before entering the crowded room. "I don't think we're going to need you for this one," a doctor told me, before stepping around me and snapping his face shield into place. I was flooded with relief.

My final shift ended. Exhausted, I emerged from the hospital onto the rooftop parking garage. The sun was just coming up over the city. I stood there and thought about this job I had just failed at. I hated being with people only in the moment of crisis, with no prior relationship and no follow-up. I hated how the only option for me in the moment was to prop up whatever beliefs they already had, even if they were terrible, destructive beliefs.

I had watched so many people deny their own pain and suffering to protect God's good reputation. Like the woman whose son was dying in front of her as she cheerfully thanked God for all the healing that was bound to come if they only had enough faith and as her husband wept angrily in the corner, longing desperately for some honesty.

I thought about all those whose pain and suffering was front and center who wanted nothing to do with God—like the woman who saw me coming down the hall for a Code Blue and screamed for me to get away from her, as though I myself were the angel of death, bringing the end to her loved one along with my prayers.

I thought about the funeral I had done—my first—for the man who was not at all religious. He was buried in his college sports team sweatshirt with a pack of cigarettes in his folded hands on the middle of his chest. His daughters, whom I had sat with alongside his body for hours after he passed, had called the hospital and asked me to do the service because he didn't like religion but they liked me. Nevertheless, when the time came, they wanted the twenty-third Psalm and "Amazing Grace" anyway. And there was something powerful for them in the "Ashes to ashes, dust to dust" ritual when I sprinkled dirt onto the coffin. I had so far to go to become comfortable with all of this, but I had come a long way.

I stood on that parking garage roof in the brisk early morning air, the sky bathing the city in pink and gold as it woke up to the day. In the distance, sandwiched between the crowded buildings, I could see church spires rising up, sprinkled around the skyline in every direction. I felt something well up inside me, a pressure in the chest, a constriction of the throat. "God," I said, to the sky and the city and the church buildings in the distance, "that is where I want to be."

"I want to be with people *before* the crisis happens, wondering together how You meet us in suffering. And I want to be with them afterward, wondering what this will mean for their life or their death. I don't want to be the triage person, with my finger in the dike, holding back the tide of sorrow by myself, filling in where the church should be. I want to be in the church, alongside others, asking together, as the church, *Where is God in this?* and helping each other navigate through."

And now here I was.

The honesty around Jo's death made it possible for us to face death with others as well. We did things more intentionally after that. At the death of longtime member Agnes, we gathered at her bedside hours before she passed and sang hymns with her husband of sixty years. When another dear saint, Lois, saw death coming near, a few close friends and I brought lemon bars, her favorite, and reminisced with her, talking with her about what she wanted at her funeral.

Death is this thing we all do alone; nobody can do that part with us. But getting to that place—we do not have to do that alone. Celebrating the incomprehensible gift of having lived, of having loved and been loved, hearing for yourself how your life has been woven into the lives of others, this is something we can do for each other. This is something we did for Jo. This is what Marty was boldly requesting.

One afternoon, in the car, during Marty's ministry among us, I was theologically outmaneuvered by a ten-year-old. It began with some offhanded, irreverent comments about death being bandied around the back seat and me gently interjecting that death was serious and not something to joke about.

One of them responded, "Why? What's the big deal?"

And I said, "Because death is final; people don't come back from that."

At which point my doctrinally astute nephew piped up, "Not always. Sometimes people *do* come back from the dead. I mean, other than Jesus, even." He then went on to tell a detailed account of his preschool teacher, who, at one point in her life, had been a missionary in another country, teaching in a school, when a bomb went off, and she died. "And God brought her back from the dead. She even has scars on her head from it," he cheerfully announced.

"Cool," Owen, eleven, declared.

(And incidentally, I happen to know this was all true, having heard the same account from my sister years before, just after having met this very teacher at my nephew's preschool.)

Before I could respond, they'd moved on to the kid from *Heaven Is for Real*, who *also* came back from the dead, and from there things kind of barreled out of reach until the next thing I knew, my whole argument was pointless, and I sat helplessly listening as they reached some kind of comfortable conclusion about death's nonfinality, because, *Hey, resurrection! Sometimes people come back!*

What happens when we die? What even is death? And what does "resurrection" have to do with all of this? One of the earliest writings in the New Testament is 1 Corinthians, dated a mere twenty-five or so years after Jesus's death and a good couple of decades before any of the Gospels. But already, despite widely circulated letters and reports, established creedal statements, and shared hymns—even despite still-living people's eyewitness accounts of the risen Jesus—this community of believers, in contrast to the kids in my car, was apparently already struggling with the idea of death's nonfinality.

What does it mean that Jesus came back from the dead? Was it "real," a *physical* resurrection of the physically dead Jesus? Or could it be some kind of *spiritual* resurrection? And what does that mean about *us*? What about our bodies and death and all that?

As Paul writes to them a letter dealing with all manner of instructions and corrections about their faith and daily life together, he saves this part for last, as though to say, *If you remember anything, you guys, remember this. This part is superimportant; the whole thing falls apart without it.* Resurrection is real. *And it matters a lot that it's real.*

Several years ago, a religious website, Patheos, ran a "one hundred word or less" feature around Easter. They asked a few people to answer something related to the resurrection, in one hundred words or less. One year the challenge was to respond to "Why I need the Resurrection." The next year it was "Is the Resurrection for real?"[1]

Paul would have really struggled with the "one hundred words or less" thing. But these two questions are the very questions he spends a whole chapter (1 Cor 15) answering. So, to get us started with the second question first, I've taken the liberty of distilling Paul's answer down to exactly one hundred words (all of them Paul's). Here is Paul (from 1 Cor 15:12–26) on the question, "Is the Resurrection for Real?"

If Christ has not been raised,
then our proclamation and your faith, have been in
    vain.
If for this life only we have hoped in Christ,
we are, of all people, most to be pitied.
If Christ has not been raised,
your faith is futile
you're still in your sins,
and those who've died in Christ have perished.
For since death came through a human being,
the resurrection of the dead has also come through
    a human being;
for as all die in Adam, so all will be made alive in
    Christ.
The last enemy to be destroyed is death.

It matters that Jesus was raised from the dead, Paul says. It *means something* that he was really raised, because he really died. His death was not figurative or conceptual; it was real. And *that* matters because *we* really die, more than a "spiritual" death. Death also has a hold on us that is something beyond simply breathing our last. It has the power to separate, to destroy, to end. There is, indeed, a finality to it.

If I had been prepared to press the argument that day in the car with my philosophical young passengers, I might have said, "Hey, kids, guess what is the one thing all those resurrected people you were talking about have in common? You know, the ones who come back from the dead like Lazarus, and your preschool teacher, and the kid from *Heaven Is for Real*—other than dying and coming back, I mean? Can you guess? They die again. Because we all die. That's how it ends. Death gets us all eventually." Boom. Final word. (Who's the smart one now, huh?)

We all die. And because we die, because death has such a hold over us, a figurative resurrection simply is not enough. Is the resurrection for real? Here, in one hundred words, was my answer:

> It had better be real.
> As real as the contractions that ripped new life from
>   my body.
> As real as the rattle that strangled life out of his.
> I've no use for a spiritual resurrection.
> If Hope
> for the drowned, damaged, disfigured, disowned,
> is emotional ease,

if the pain of flesh and bones
is answered with mystical comfort,
if Guns are stronger than god,
then count me out.
But tell me that Death Loses,
tell me that Life Prevails,
and not in the abstract,
but in pulsing blood, flowing tears, thumping heart,
then the Resurrection
is Hope
for us all.[2]

The Bible and our Christian faith are full of paradoxes. Jesus is both completely human and completely God. God is One God who is at the same time simultaneously Father, Son, and Spirit. We are a vast variety of uncontrollably different people, and yet we are also somehow one body, suffering and rejoicing with each other. And this is the biggie, which the Corinthians were having a hard time getting their head around: *we die—our lives end—but also, death is not the end.*

The paradox starts with something Paul wants us to recognize about death: Death is two different things at the same time. On the one hand, it is the inevitable and natural end of earthly life, the cessation of breathing and heartbeat and brain activity. Part of living on the earth means we die. This reality is shared by all creatures—plants, animals, and humans. That is one meaning of death.

But that is not the *sting* of death. The sting of death is sin (1 Cor 15:56), which is to say, it is separation—separation from God, separation from those we love, separation from our true connection and fullness, from all the beauty and joy of living, from the ongoing creativity and unfolding projects we are just in the middle of, from the time that isn't long enough and the relationships that are just getting going. Separation, division, destruction. That's sin.

Sin means death reaches into all of life, wreaking havoc on the earth, inside us, between us. Death as separation brings anguish, despair, and torment. It lurks in our weak and perishable bodies, clinging to our mortality and frailty, feeding our shame and judgment. It preys on our fears, whispering that these things can keep us from one another, can keep us from God, can keep us from love, can prevent us from being worthy of receiving love or capable of giving love. From all that is real and good and true and essential to our being, sin gives death the authority to regularly, ultimately, and permanently separate us.

But here is the good news, Paul says (in many, many words): Jesus Christ defeated death. "Listen, I will tell you a mystery! We will not all die, but we will all be changed, in a moment, in the twinkling of an eye, at the last trumpet" (1 Cor 15:51–52). And then he says, "For this perishable body must put on imperishability, and this mortal body must put on immortality. . . . Then the saying that is written will be fulfilled:

'Death has been swallowed up in victory.'
'Where, O death, is your victory?
Where, O death, is your sting?'" (1 Cor 15:53–55)

Death doesn't have the power to separate us forever—and although the separation we experience now with death is frightening and real, it is temporary and restricted, because resurrection exists in Christ's body and one day will exist in us too. Christ has come from outside death, from the time when all will live, into this time when all will die. God has broken through that barrier of immortality and imperishability, and taken onto Godself mortality and weakness, joining us inside this whole dying kind of living thing.

And now that Christ has died, with us and for us, and has risen, bodily, from the dead, he brings us with him out of this time when all will die, into the time when all will live, the time of resurrection and new life. We perishable beings will put on imperishability; we mortal beings will put on immortality.

In the very, very end, life—unbroken connection to God and each other in love—is what triumphs. Death's reign is broken, and my kids' baptism mantra, which guarded them against nightmares in their younger years, is powerful and true: "Death can't get me, because Jesus has got me."

And it also means death as a natural part of living doesn't have the power to end us. When we wear out and stop breathing and *being*, in the way we understand being, nevertheless we go on. The end of our human journey here on earth is simply a transition from one chapter to the next, a shift to the new way of being, moving us from the time when all die to the time when all live. Death dies. Life lasts.

This life after death is not hypothetical or spiritual; it is real and bodily and true. It embraces and transforms the whole of us, not just some disembodied soul part that separates from the rest of us and floats off. And this eternal life is for more than just us; it is for the whole earth, the ravaged oceans and decimated mountains and flooded valleys. It is for the stolen children and the grieving parents, the abused generations and war-torn nations, the systemically oppressed, the poor and the privileged—for all the broken promises and broken hearts. In the very, very end, all things will be redeemed and made new.

Biblical scholar Richard Carlson states that "the ultimate theological question for Paul is not: 'What happens to us when we die?' Rather, the ultimate theological question is, 'Who has final say regarding the existence of everything in the cosmos, Death or God?' Paul's answer is clear: At Christ's [second coming] the final victory will belong to God as humanity marked by Christ will be raised; Christ will destroy all that stands in opposition to God; and Christ will hand over everything he has liberated back to God so that God will be the everything in everything (1 Corinthians 15:24–28)."[3]

God has the final say: not death; life. And if that is true—and we are banking all on the trust that it is—then *thanks be to God, who gives us the victory through our Lord Jesus Christ!* Because nothing is futile or wasted. Nothing is hopeless or lost.

All the things that separate and divide, degrade and destroy, their power is temporary; their end is ensured. But every act and word and prayer and thought that comes from love returns to love. It is part of what endures forever. Every moment of forgiveness and connection, every building up and reaching out, each experience of devotion and care remains eternally, because love never fails.

So Paul's words to the Corinthians are meant for us too: "Therefore, my beloved, be steadfast, immovable, always excelling in the work of the Lord, because you know that in the Lord your labor is not in vain" (1 Cor 15:58).

The true hope of death's nonfinality is not that some people here and there might escape death to come back for a few more years before succumbing again. (Sorry, kids.) And it's not that we have cracked the mystery of what happens after each of us dies, or that we have been given a spiritual comfort in figurative ideas to get us through life. The hope of the resurrection is that the question of who has the final say over the whole cosmos has been settled, once and for all. And nothing matters more than that.

So why do I need the resurrection? In the summer of 2016, here was my hundred-word answer:[4]

> I need the Resurrection
> because this week
> my foster niece came back with a broken arm,
> and last night my daughter learned
> that not all Amber Alerts have happy endings.
> I need the Resurrection
> because Marty's on his way and we can't stop it,
> and little Omran's brother didn't survive the blast
>   after all.
> Because I've detonated rage
> and watched their sweet faces harden and close to me.
> Because evil is pervasive
> and I participate.
> I need the Resurrection
> because it promises

that in the end
all wrongs are made right.
Death loses.
Hope triumphs.
And Life and Love
Prevail.

And here, distilled into exactly one hundred words—from his letter to the Romans (8:31–40)—is Paul's answer to "Why I Need the Resurrection":

What then are we to say about these things?
If God is for us, who's against us?
Who will separate us from the love of Christ?
Will hardship, distress, persecution?
Will famine, or nakedness, or peril, or sword?
No, in all these things
we are more than conquerors
through him who loved us.
For I'm convinced
that neither death, nor life,
nor angels, nor rulers,
nor things present, nor things to come,
nor powers,
nor height, nor depth,
nor anything else in all creation,
will be able to separate us
from the love of God in Christ Jesus our Lord.

Marty was sad about dying and sometimes a little scared about how his last moments would go. But he was not afraid of death. He said he believed that what comes next is just love. We simply dissolve into the enduring and all-encompassing love of God. I could see that this idea settled and moved him. He liked the thought of letting go of this life and disappearing into the substance of love. Then he asked me what I thought happens when we die.

Love is our source and our destination. But in Christ, God has claimed as beloved each individual, unique person. Our earthly lives matter to God. And when we die, nothing of who we are will be lost. I answered Marty that I thought it would be a gathering up rather than a melting down. Somehow, even as we are completely joined in love, our unique selves will continue in the unencumbered communion of all selves. We will exist in complete belonging. We will experience complete connection, without barrier or division. There will be fulfillment and wholeness brought to all that was left unsettled, unfinished, incomplete, or damaged in each one of us in this life. This life is not forgotten, I told him. It's not rendered pointless. It's made complete. We are swept up into the whole, yes. But the whole of who we each are, alongside each other, is brought forever into the eternal love of God.

"That sounds really nice, Kara," he said. "I'm going to have to think more about that."

Chapter 10

When We Surrender to Our Nothingness

———◆———

It was easy to love God in all that was beautiful. The lesson of deeper knowledge, though, instructed me to embrace God in all things.

—SAINT FRANCIS OF ASSISI,
The Writings of St. Francis of Assisi

All shall be well . . . for there is a force of love moving through the universe that holds us fast and will never let us go.

—JULIAN OF NORWICH, *All Will Be Well*

The more the insight that life is surprising takes hold of us, the more our life will be a life of hope, a life of openness for Surprise. And Surprise is a name for God. In fact, Surprise is a somewhat more successful name for God than others, though all names miss the mark when we aim at naming the Nameless One.

—BR. DAVID STEINDL-RAST,
Gratefulness, the Heart of Prayer

April 2017

*A*s winter melted away and spring began to surface in tiny green shoots poking through the crusty ice and mud, Marty's breathing became much more labored. He was still taking a walk around the lake every day. His outings used to be an hour long; some days now they were only ten minutes. Then that too became hard. He could feel the end coming nearer. Finally, one day the call came that I was anticipating. "Kara, I am ready." It was time for Marty's service.

Unlike Jo, Marty wanted his service to be a goodbye, straight up. There was to be no avoiding the fact, no awkward "Bon voyage" for Marty. We called the gathering "Saying Goodbye: An Evening of Storytelling, Gratitude and Love for Marty." The invitation read,

> Life is full of goodbyes. Short ones, long ones, casual ones, deep ones, goodbyes that come too soon, and those that go on for a long time. Goodbyes release us with a blessing—sharing how much we mean to each other and that we will be missed. And goodbyes are important. Sometimes we don't get them, and sometimes we do. And sometimes we make a big, wonderful to-do of it . . .

This special evening with Marty, we will eat delicious food, laugh, probably cry, tell stories about
Marty, thank God for Marty, and thank Marty for
sharing life with us.

The preparation for the evening was a labor of love. The
service was to be followed by a meal—all of Marty's favorite
foods. We ordered lasagna and salad from his favorite Ital-
ian restaurant, and all sorts of people prepared a shocking
amount of cherry pies and apple cobblers. We filled the gathering room with gorgeously bedecked tables draped in light
blue—Marty's favorite color—and set with fancy dishes.

When the evening came, the sanctuary gradually filled
up with church members, Marty's sister and brother, and his
"bar friends," most of whom sat together on one side of the
sanctuary like wedding guests. We had put out a chair for him,
as we had done for Jo, but Marty didn't want to sit alone in the
center. Instead, he sat in the pew with his friends, one of
the crowd.

Tied onto flagpoles, a rope stretched from one side of the
front to the other, filled with clothespins. At the entrance to
the sanctuary, we placed a stack of 8.5″ × 14″ paper and a pile
of colored markers on a table. The sheets of paper had printed
on them in large font, "Marty is . . ." with room for people to
finish the sentence.

Just before the service, Marty pulled me aside and told
me his stomach had been bad that day. He said he might have
to get up in the middle of the service to use the bathroom, and
he asked if I would please make that announcement before the
service began. I felt great awe and tenderness standing there

in the hallway with that request in my hands. That he was so comfortable in his humanity, so at home in his vulnerability, that he would ask me to tell a sanctuary full of people that he had diarrhea was somehow so poignant and beautiful to me, I had to catch my breath before I headed inside.

I welcomed everyone, shared Marty's requested announcement, and told them we were here to tell stories, to celebrate Marty's life, to affirm our presence with him as he moved closer to his death, and to remind him that in life and in death, he belongs to God.

As Marty's favorite song, "What a Wonderful World," rang out in Jeanne's clear, gentle voice, I felt the lump in my chest work its way up to my face, and I began to cry. This felt too hard. It felt impossible. How would we survive what we were about to do? I looked across from me at the rows of Marty's bar friends who were also crying, strangers weeping alongside church members and me. This whole big roomful of people brought together by our love for Marty was crying together. They, too, looked scared. Maybe we were not going to make it through this thing.

But something incredible happens in these experiences of confronting our fear and sticking with the discomfort. It's excruciating, yes, but that only lasts a moment. Once we go through the death part together, refusing to let it have the final word, we come out the other side a little bit unshakable. We experience a different kind of invincibility from what the world offers, or even the kind I had grown up believing faith to be about. This invincibility comes through weakness. It's an invulnerability found only through utter vulnerability.[1]

Sitting in the death experience together made us able to face whatever all this was with gratitude, sadness, and love. And most astounding of all, without fear.

So we all stuck with it and stayed put through the excruciating part, crying into our tissues and not leaving. We didn't let the difficulty define or dissuade us. We simply felt our way through it. On the other side, we discovered freedom.

The song ended, and I rose and walked to the podium. I said, "Hear these words from Scripture: 'Since we are surrounded by so great a cloud of witnesses, let us also lay aside every weight and the sin that clings so closely, and let us run with perseverance the race that is set before us, looking to Jesus the pioneer and perfecter of our faith, who for the sake of the joy that was set before him endured the cross, disregarding its shame, and has taken his seat at the right hand of the throne of God'" (Heb 12:1–2).

I continued,

One year and three days ago, we commissioned Marty to a Ministry of Dying. Marty said yes to a form of leadership by example, a willingness to share his journey with us and let us share this time with him. His charge was not to put on a good attitude or wow us with his witty wisdom and end-of-life insight. He promised simply to be honest and true, not to hide his pain or questions, but to allow us to share in them with him.

And we vowed to share this journey with him, to laugh with him and cry with him, to look backward and forward together, and mostly to be right here in whatever each "right here" brings. We said, where Marty goes, we will go, and we will be his people (Ruth 1:16) alongside him in this journey as far as we can accompany him, until he takes the final steps with Christ alone, into the everlasting arms of God's love.

Marty is joining the great cloud of witnesses, and today we are witnessing to his impact on our lives. Whenever someone joins this congregation, I say to them that we all will change—because all a congregation is, is the people here. We are made up of all the personalities and passions, struggles and doubts, life stories and hopes, fears and dreams of everyone who shows up, as we minister to each other the love of God.

Marty has ministered to all of us God's love. He once told me, "We are here on earth to take care of each other." And not only is that how he has lived in the world, taking care of others, but he has created that ministry in this community. He has allowed us to take care of him on this journey. We are learning how to take care of each other because of you, Marty. We are learning what it means to belong to one another, because you have belonged to us.

Then I gestured to the clothesline and the papers at the back of the sanctuary and continued: "So today we get to witness back to Marty who he is, and what he means to us.

Each of you is invited to come up with your sign, share what it says, and tell us a little something that goes along with it, a story, quote, memory, description of or gratitude for Marty. Then you can hang up your sign, and the next person can share. You do not have to come share. You can write Marty a note, speak to him later, or just witness by your presence here today your gratitude and love for Marty."

Then I went first. I held up the sign I had completed, "Marty is . . . surprising." I said, "Marty comes across as unassuming and unpretentious. He's not flashy or attention grabbing; he might blend into the background if you didn't know him. One of my favorite moments of this whole year was when I got to hear Marty's life story. Underneath his humble exterior, Marty is an adventurer. He's a lover of life, explorer, seeker of new experiences and knowledge."

"Who here has snorkeled shipwrecks in the Great Lakes? Raise your hand." Marty's hand went up. "Been a Buddhist?" A few hands. "Wiccan?" just Marty's, accompanied by a sprinkling of laughter. "Who here has worked as a private eye?" Again Marty's hand went up, he was grinning widely now, and people were laughing. "Is certified as a health care administrator?" Marty's hand. "Has skied all over the mountains of Colorado, Utah, Northern Idaho, and Jackson Hole?" Marty's hand. The whole room was watching him, and he was beaming. I continued.

"Raise your hand if you've lived in Colombia for two years? Who here has a reputation as an excellent astrologer? Who has worked with troubled teens through the county court system? Trained as an acupuncturist?"

Marty's hand bounced up and down, and I watched the roomful of people light up in delight as this man we all loved claimed his one wild, wonderful, and surprising life right before our eyes.

"See what I mean!?" I continued. "The more you know him, the more there is to discover!"

Then I looked right at Marty and said,

I love you, Marty. I love being your pastor. I love getting to know you. I love how you care for others and contribute to community and share your gifts and yourself. How you jump into things and learn them, how you step down when you're finished. I love your election button collection. And how well you know yourself and what you need and stand up for that.

You have taught me about living with courage, integrity, and gratitude, and I am thankful beyond words that I have gotten to be church with you, caring for each other. You didn't have to do that. You could have kept all this to yourself and borne it alone. But you didn't. You put your money where your mouth is on the whole caring-for-each-other thing and you let us be there for you and with you. Thank you, Marty.

I made my way back to my pew and sat down. A moment later someone else rose, then others followed, taking turns coming to the front to share. I watched Marty's bar friends, some of whom were decidedly not church people, and his church friends, some of whom were decidedly not bar people, become bound together in our love for Marty. We were opened up in our view of him, deepened in our gratitude for him. We were witnessing together the incredible impact of a single, ordinary life that ripples through us and beyond.

Marty is . . . Kind. Brave. Gentle. A gift. A friend. Hopeful. Loving. Welcoming. Children shared. Friends from elementary school shared. People who hadn't planned to share shared. We glimpsed seasons of his life before many of us knew him, like Marty the hippy, and Marty the one they were *certain* was an FBI agent. We saw parts of Marty we wouldn't have known, like Marty who loved espresso martinis and held the bartender accountable for making a good one. Marty, who believed we are here on this earth to take care of each other, was teaching us in this very moment how to do that by letting us take care of him.

We, too, are the great cloud of witnesses. We got to reflect back to Marty, who he was, his true identity: *Beloved. Child of God.* Beyond the sickness or the dying, even beyond all he'd done and been in this world, we got to remind him who he was, by sharing from our own experience of his person, our own encounters with his being. And so we were the voice of God to him.

Then I preached a short message to this group, but mostly to Marty.

We have a great cloud of witnesses—together and each of us in our own lives, people whose time here on earth has forever shaped our own journeys, who have, by living their lives, left a trail, a remnant of themselves in the world that makes us all more able to run our own races, people we can imagine cheering us on from beyond, rooting for us, always in our corner. Marty is one of those.

But also we have a God who has taken this same road, who came into the life alongside us, with all our weaknesses and fears, and took on all that separates us from God, that which dehumanizes and divides us, which we sometimes call sin. All the pain and sorrow we endure in this life, God took into Godself and bore even the greatest separation of all, which is death. And Christ died for us, and rose again, so that nothing might ever separate us from the love we were made from and made for and return to.

This life will end, but love will continue, Marty will continue in love. This is not the end. Love never ends. And once we've shared love, there is no way to go back. Marty will always be a part of us, and we him. For having known you, loved you, belonged to you as your people, we will never be the same, Marty. Thank you for sharing your life with us.

When I finished my sermon-to-one, we gathered around him—those of us who were praying people—and laid our hands on him and prayed for him once more: *Ease his pain. . . . Fill him with peace. . . . Hold him in love and grace in these coming days. . . . Bless him.*

And then, just as we had done when we commissioned him to a Ministry of Dying one year and three days before, we anointed Marty with the sign of the cross on his forehead. This time we told him that his baptism would soon be complete.

"Do not be afraid," I said. "Life and love are where you come from, and they are where you are going. We will walk with you to the point where you go on alone. And you go on with Christ, who goes with you, because always and forever, you belong to God."

As one, bound together by that thing that happens when love outlasts fear, hearts full to bursting, we all left the sanctuary and flowed across the hall to fill the "gathering room," where the feast awaited. Gentle conversation surrounded us like music. The room rang with laughter and ease, warmth and care. Life abundant, life overflowing and free. Many of Marty's friends came up to thank me and to tell me they were pondering other stories, or they had ideas for ways to bless him, or they were so glad to be part of this special evening.

I was conscious in that moment of the nearly palpable sense that we were all held inside something together, something precious and true and unknowable. We felt connected. Awake. Cleansed. Grace, transcendence, holiness filled the room. We had stepped out of the ordinary and into the sacred. We had stopped, and God had met us right there. And, over cherry pie and apple cobbler, God was meeting us still.

James Finley used to go to writer, monk, and activist Father Thomas Merton for spiritual direction. When he arrived, Merton would ask him, "How's it going?" If Finley answered, "It's going well!" Merton would respond, "Don't worry, before too long it won't be going so well." And if he answered, "It's not going so well," Merton would respond, "Don't worry, before too long, it will be going well."[2]

You aren't sleeping through the night? Don't worry; soon your kid will be done teething. You are sleeping through the night? Don't worry; soon your kid will be out driving late at night with friends. You are stable and happy and healthy and have a job you love? Don't worry; before too long you'll get sick, or lose your job, or face some financial hardship. You are going through a difficult illness, hunting for a new job, or struggling to make ends meet? Don't worry; before too long your treatment will be finished, you will find employment, and one day you will finish paying off your student loans.

In Luke 6:17–38 (part of the Sermon on the Plain, containing Luke's version of Matthew's Beatitudes), Jesus is among a crowd of people in what sounds like an overwhelming scene: a massive gathering from the whole region, pressing in on him, trying to touch him because power is going out from him and people are being healed of all sorts of ills. In the middle of this scene Jesus looks up at his disciples, and he gives them this sermon.

First, he pronounces a collection of blessings and woes, which is to say a litany of "How good you have it!" and "Sucks to be you!" *How good you have it, you who are poor, or hungry, or weeping, or when people say terrible things about you. You should leap for joy, for yours is the kingdom of God, you will be fed, you will laugh, and you are in good company. And you who are rich and full and happy? Sucks to be you, for all of that will disappear, and you'll be left with nothing.*

Whatever it is that we look to for security and stability, comfort and ease, the things we assume are defining and sustaining our lives, they are fickle and changing, as Marty had come to know acutely. Ability or disability, health or illness, weakness or strength, beauty or cruelty, happiness or despair, our lives cycle through it all, and we don't ever stop and stay somewhere, as though we've arrived. So even though we like to imbue them with power, they don't actually determine reality. There must be something else, something greater, something deeper than this that holds us. We must rest our souls, our security, our trust, in something or someone more than what we feel and experience.

But here's what's so difficult about this: we don't get there through strength. When we avoid our pain, pretend what someone said doesn't hurt, prop ourselves up with our assets and gifts and our "at leasts"—*at least I have my health, at least I have friends, at least I'm not as bad off as they are*—we give those things power over us, and we become trapped by the pain, captive to the messages, enslaved to do everything possible to preserve ourselves and at least not lose our *at leasts*. We cannot be free. But that doesn't stop us from doing everything we can to avoid the nothingness.

The real life, the real security, the real hope is found in our weakness. When you know nothingness, you will be ministered to by God. When you don't try to flee it or avoid it, but acknowledge it and even receive it, you will find that the God who comes to us as minister will minister to you.

Marty was no longer avoiding his nothingness. He was right up against his impossibility. And when we went there with him by choosing to say goodbye, we faced the horror of his—and so also our own—death, together. And there God ministered to us.

My friend Phil teaches the Enneagram in prisons. He gathers with groups of prisoners who want to talk about what unthought responses and defense mechanisms typical of their personality types trap them and get them into trouble. When he first started teaching it, he kept marveling about how receptive the prisoners were and how dramatic the changes in them were once they started recognizing their patterns. These are people living right up against their impossibility. They have no illusions about their weakness. Their gut reactions and unthought responses have *clearly* not worked out for them. He said, "They are so much freer than I am. They have nothing more to lose and no illusions about their own imprisonment. I get to walk around feeling like I'm doing pretty well. My defense mechanisms are working out, thank you very much. I get to pretend I am not trapped in my own ego and cut off from real connection and relationships."

So how good it is to be you when things aren't working out so well, because you can confess your death and be met by life. And sucks to be you when you're doing a good job escaping your nothingness and deluding yourself that you've got it handled, because your death is going to come as something of a shock. How good it is to be you who can embrace your nothingness. And sucks to be you who believe you can escape it. That's the first part of Jesus's sermon. And I like to imagine that the chaos has died down a little bit around him, and people are straining to eavesdrop as he continues talking to his disciples, because as hard as that must have been to hear, he then ups the ante.

The part Jesus says next would get a lot of clapback on Twitter. Social media is a perfect medium for people to destroy each other. The extraordinary speed and venom with which we can soundly condemn someone are matched only by how impossible it feels to achieve redemption once you've been condemned. So imagine how Jesus's message would go over with us: *Bless those who curse you! Love your enemies! Don't just love those who love you; that's meaningless. Love those who hate you! Reach out to those who've rejected you from their tribe. Pray for those who abuse you. When someone does something terribly hurtful to you, deserving to feel the same sting they've inflicted on you and the pain they've caused you, don't give it back. Instead, show them mercy, pray for them, be kind to them. Share your stuff with the people who don't return it. Lend to those who may not repay you. Big deal if you can be good to those who are good to you. So you engage in an economy of trading and bartering things and emotions and respect; what does that prove? Anybody can do that,* he says (Luke 6:27–34).

Weirdly, God is *kind* to the ungrateful and wicked. We'd much rather see the ungrateful and wicked taken down a few notches. In fact, we'll gladly do that ourselves. We'll call them out, shred their reputations, give them one star, and call them trash. We will make them pay for their ingratitude and wickedness. But Jesus says, *Live in God's mercy and extend it to others. Live in God's forgiveness and extend it to others. Live in God's grace and extend it to others. Especially when they don't merit it. That's when it really matters. Don't judge, and you won't be judged. Don't condemn, and you won't be condemned. Forgive, and you'll be forgiven. Give, and it will be given to you. Trust in God's reality where there is enough—enough love and forgiveness and grace and hope—and where we are not heaping judgment and condemnation on each other and ourselves. Live this way, and this is how you will live. Rest in this reality. Return to the deepest belonging.*

The only way to move from the way of fear to the way of God is through death and resurrection. Die to yourself and to all you thought might keep you safe or make you invincible or good or immune. Die to what you thought was giving you life. *You're always stuck in impossibility*, Jesus tells us, *so surrender.*

When you surrender, you get your humanity back. Marty and the prisoners learning the Enneagram dismantled their own defenses or had them torn down and let their lives be transformed. They knew something the rest of us don't: when you've surrendered to your nothingness and embraced your death, you are no longer ruled by it. And when you are not ruled by your death—when you are not fleeing it, denying it, avoiding it—you will not be overtaken by comparison or consumed by jealousy. You will not need to prove yourself better than or equal to others. You will not need to get caught in defensiveness and retaliation. *You will be free.*

Everything we do in life is an attempt to escape nothingness. We're terrified by it, obsessed with it. It's why Adam and Eve ate the apple, and it's why we tweet. We want to build our own somethingness and fiercely uphold it. *But if you're my disciple*, Jesus says, *walk right into nothingness. Walk into your weakness and surrender to it. Lay down your life, and you will find it.*

Live with your nothingness. Right up against your nothingness is where you'll find the love and grace, the mercy and forgiveness of God. Right up against your nothingness is where you'll find *freedom*. You can't kill what's already dead, the Apostle Paul reminds us. And we are those who have died and been raised into new life with Christ. We are those pulled into the love of God—the love *in* God, inside the very being of

God—the love of the Father to the Son by the Spirit. The grace of God inside the Trinity spills out into the world to create and claim us, as beloved, in God's own image, and God ministers to us in our need.

If this is where we begin—already in our nothingness and impossibility—then we cannot be pulled into the game of creating our own somethingness and defending our own possibility. This, too, is why we rest, why we Sabbath. We return to our nothingness, where God begins *ex nihilo*, "out of nothing," to create us again. It is in our nothingness—our poverty and hunger and sadness and death—that God comes to us and gives us back our humanity. And it is here that we minister to each other. Giving and receiving love and care, we live out the image of God. God puts us in communion with God and each other, to rediscover our true belonging, the hesed that is at the core of it all—to return to the love and belongingness we most deeply long for and that we recognize in our deepest self when we experience it.

All around us the lie is going to continue to holler that we are apart and against and there's only enough belonging for some, and only enough respect for a few, and the winners will win, and the losers will lose. But at the core of everything is God's grace and mercy. And the world God made, and has redeemed us for, is one of deep connection and love. We get there through death, not apart from it. Instead of protecting ourselves from being hurt, or trying to create and uphold our own possibility in the world, we surrender. Surrender to the stop and rest, surrender to the impossibility and the inability to save ourselves. There we find our salvation.

The time is coming when nobody will be hungry or poor or sick, when everyone will have enough, and when nobody will be less than, discarded, or overlooked. This is God's reality; it is as things are meant to be and will one day be for good. It is where we all will one day stop and stay. We join in it now.

Then, beyond the game and the illusion and the constant striving and comparing, we are participating in the deepest belonging. We are living the real reality. We are acting as though we belong to one another *because we do*. Jesus says to treat someone as worthy of respect, even if they don't deserve it. If someone takes your coat, give your shirt too. Give *more* than is demanded unfairly of you. Upset the applecart. Be the one who sets the terms. Don't react and keep track. Die to that way of life, and rise to a different way of being. Refuse to be divided by other people's actions or words. Refuse to let them make you reject them. Refuse to let their pain, or rage, or hatred, or vitriol set the terms for how you will treat them.

Instead of strong, be weak. Instead of wary, be generous. Treat people as more deserving of kindness than they generally are, says Jesus, who right as he is saying it is also doing it—*showing* kindness, without distinction, liberally healing all those who come near. They touch him, and they're healed. They don't even have to ask the right way, or show they've earned it, or be a good person, or have the right religion, or turn their life around and use it for good. Jesus is just healing them, because it's who Jesus is. It's what God does.

Jesus is standing in a sea of broken and longing people, very few of them deserving at the moment—and those who are deserving won't be for long—people who are mostly confused, mostly unkind to each other, people who are lost and frantic to escape their nothingness, people not unlike you and me and all those we know. And he's just giving out healing and hope willy-nilly, without prescreening or checking credentials. And in the midst of this madness, he's gathering those of us who are longing to follow and are willing to be sent, and he is inviting us to face our own nothingness.

He's telling us to embrace our own impossibility, to recognize the futility of our reliance on anything to save us—be it goodness or health or wisdom or financial security or reputation or hard work or people's praise and good opinions of us—because just wait, tomorrow it will be gone. He's inviting us to live as though we are already dead, which is to be truly alive. Our ground of being cannot be shaken, because it extends deeper than the things that come and go on the surface. We are being rooted and grounded in love (Eph 3:17). We are being held and upheld in God.

And then he's giving these ludicrous instructions, these self-emptying instructions. These *ministry* instructions. *Be merciful like God who is merciful, who empties Godself to take on the form of a human being and come right in alongside us.* So we empty ourselves and go toward the nothingness and impossibility inside of us and others. We let our utter vulnerability make us invulnerable to destruction, let our weakness become the strength to go right in alongside each other where Jesus is.

Go toward each other, make the kind of relationships where people are seen and heard. Live the deeper truth. Live the wider hope. Live the greater mercy. Show forgiveness—a rare, upsetting, and potent thing these days. Live in grace—share in God's fullness and contribute to others' fullness. Surrender to God, who surrenders to us, and then surrender to each other. Come alongside each other as God comes alongside us. Be ministers. Let God set you free. The life in you will be contagious. Luke 6:38 says, "A good measure, pressed down, shaken together, running over, will be put into your lap; for the measure you give will be the measure you get back." Life will be returned to you when you don't expect it; it will be a filled-up, bubbling-over kind of infectious life. Live this way, and you will be truly alive.

Chapter 11

When Grace Tells Our Story

———◆———

I have found the paradox, that if you love until
it hurts, there can be no more hurt, only more
love.

—DAPHNE RAE, *Love until It Hurts*
(widely misattributed to Mother Teresa)

All life holds within itself a promise of resurrection.
—GABRIEL MARCEL, *The Mystery of Being*

May 2017

Marty and Nancy had reconnected shortly before his
diagnosis. She'd been an old friend; they had first
met in kindergarten. In the past year, as he grew sicker and
sicker, improbably, Marty and Nancy had fallen in love. In this
liminal time when Marty was suspended in between life and

death, this astounding, unexpected gift had been bestowed upon him—his relationship with Nancy. Knowing his end was near, and not wanting to cause her to suffer, it took Marty some time and courage to receive this gift fully. "How can I let her come close if I am just going to leave her?" he asked me once.

"I think she knows that, Marty. And I think she can decide for herself what she can handle," I answered. And she could. Nancy was brave, gentle, and steady, not scared off by Marty's suffering.

Marty's fear made sense to me, though. Suffering makes us vulnerable, and sharing vulnerability can be terrifying. Suffering seems like it will cut us off from people, as though suffering makes us uniquely unable to enter the human story. In the way of fear, suffering is nothing but alienating. But it's not the suffering that is powerful; it's the fear—the dread of infecting others with pain, or the sense that, infected ourselves, we're unworthy or unable to connect with others. It's the resistance to suffering that does damage, not the suffering itself.

Yes, suffering makes us vulnerable. But vulnerability makes us beautiful. It draws people in. Our vulnerability calls out to their vulnerability, our humanity to theirs. Suffering is meant to be shared; we are meant to share it with each other. Shared suffering is nothing like suffering alone. It doesn't spread and infect like a virus, as fear would have us believe. Shared suffering connects and strengthens and emboldens. In some bizarre paradox, sharing suffering sets us free.

Shared suffering is a sacred thing, because we all suffer, we're all vulnerable, and we're all connected. Sharing suffering just makes the truth of our deepest belonging come to the surface; it moves us out of alienation and into interdependence. The most direct way to move out of the way of fear and back into the way of God is to share suffering.

Maybe Nancy knew that. Or maybe she just cared too much about Marty to keep away. She had lost both her parents in the previous two years, so perhaps she was already familiar with the grace of living so close to our humanity. Maybe she was even further along than Marty, already knowing something about this life-right-up-next-to-death stuff. In any case, Nancy signed on to join with Marty on his journey to the grave, because that was where he was going, like it or not, and she wanted to be with him. Of course she would have preferred he live. Of course she wished that their future together could have looked radically different. But she took what she could get, which was enough.

Marty finally let Nancy in. He let her see and share his suffering. He let her see him at his weakest, his worst. He did not have strength to offer her. Not lightness or ease. Not a future. There were no illusions about where this was going—or not going, as the case may be. When sickness and nausea, pain and insomnia, decline and loss shape our days, we must make ourselves incredibly vulnerable to let someone be in that with us. He did, and now Nancy was by Marty's side nearly every moment. He told me that he would have liked to marry her. He would have liked the chance to make a life with Nancy. And in a way, he did. Here they were, spending the rest of his life together.

Witnessing Marty in that liminal place was a gift. It's important to say that Marty was not a saint. The gift was his ordinariness, his just-like-the-rest-of-us-ness. Trusting in his belonging to God was not always easy. Sometimes fear overtook him and trust felt impossible. He knew God was with him—he remembered and forgot. We knew God was with us—we remembered and forgot. He reminded us; we reminded him. In grace, God joins us and ministers to us, and we, made in God's image, are made to join and minister to each other. This dance of grace carried us through. *We belong to God. We belong to each other. Jesus is right here with us. We are not afraid. Lord, help our fear.*

Grace means that at any and every moment, God has already restored us to our orientation toward the Source of our life, and we can receive this reality, and rest in it. But to receive it, and allow the Holy Spirit to reorient us to our Source, means we must let go of whatever we have been orienting ourselves toward instead. We must release our grip on the wheel. We've been aiming our lives toward our own self-interest and self-preservation, our righteous anger or longing for revenge, the isolation or blame that makes the people around us into competitors instead of companions, and the fruitless efforts of grasping for meaning apart from the Source of our being.

All the things that make us feel safe and strong and secure and worthy must disappear. They are the illness, the sin, that distorts our true life, our true connection to God and each other. But nobody—or at least, not most people I know—willingly gives up safety and strength. Certainly, I know I don't. Would you willingly give up security? Stability? The ability to trust in your own good health, or reliable mind, or excellent track record, or reputation in the world? And so we are rarely ready to receive grace until suffering meets us.

Until we are freed, often against our will, from something that we depend on for what we thought was our life, we are not likely to be grateful for grace or even able to see it at work, which is another way of saying, *We don't really recognize or think we need God.*

Often, only when what we thought was our life disappears, only in death—and these deaths happen to everyone all the time—are we ready to discover and receive again what truly is our life: our deep and abiding and unshakable belonging to God and to all others. And so Marty lived in grace, close to grace. And to be near him was to be near grace.

To know grace is to taste the awareness that all of life is a gift, that we ourselves are a gift to others, and that each experience—the painful ones included—turns out to be a gift as well. To know grace is the consciousness that there is deeper truth and greater hope and stronger love that can be received only in vulnerability and weakness. Grace makes us awake to life, brave to love, able to forgive, willing to sacrifice, free from shame and fear, quick to joy, and receptive to peace.

Sometime around twenty years after my family fell apart, I was sitting outside a coffee shop, journal open and pen in hand, waiting for my own kids to walk past me on their way home from school so I could join them. The sun was shining, the sky was bright blue, and the air was perfect, soft and warm. I had slipped into daydreaming, and with a start, I awoke to a stunning realization.

By then, all four of Andy's and my parents had partnered for the long haul with other people, who had adult kids of their own. Their attention and energy were poured into the new lives they'd built, and we'd had years of juggling all the complications that blending (or not, as the case may be) new families brings.

My sisters and I had all settled where we'd scattered, and we'd all formed new families of our own. Eventually, all three of my sisters had finished college—courageously, in their thirties, with kids underfoot. Our parents had each remarried, and they became loving, long-distance grandparents to our kids, and we were given the grace of relating through new definitions and roles. Tumult is tenacious, and our generation has its own share of brokenness and new beginnings. Our relating is occasionally rich, and often fraught. It's bittersweet, filled with love and longing, and never easy. But we love each other. And that will never change.[1]

In the early years, the anger had been enormous. At one point, Mollie, who had let me walk alongside her when she felt what it was to be separated from family by one's choices, advised me to be gracious with my dad. "he loves you all so much! how afraid he must feel, keeping all those secrets!" I gradually surrendered my way into grace, and I feel it holding me even now. But I had to feel the anger first. So, while I wrestled with my own loss of faith and crisis of truth, Mollie supported me in letters and phone calls, just as I had done for her.

The passing of time gifts us with new capacities to be in the present, if we choose. And when we do, the past finds its place, and healing happens. Over time I forged new relationships with my parents and siblings that continue to evolve, along with the circumstances of life. But despite everything, for a very long time, the defining fulcrum of my story was the break. The fracturing of my family was *the* big event that shaped me.

But that day on the cafe patio, with the sun shining down, and the anticipation of my own dear little ones bouncing up the sidewalk in their bouncing up the sidewalk in their backpacks, quite suddenly I realized my family's collapse *was no longer my life's most defining experience*. My life has been filled with so much joy and wonder, so much intention and purpose, so much beauty and redemption. *That* is what defines my life. My family's destruction is part of my story, certainly, a valuable part, but it is not the biggest part. Being a mom is bigger. Being married to Andy is bigger. Even pastoring a congregation is a bigger part of my story, a more prominent melody line in the intricate song of my life. I am who I am today because of what has happened to me—all of it.

And even more than the realization that the break no longer loomed largest was the astonishing realization that I felt *gratitude* for what had happened. My capacity for trust, my dependence on God, my courage, and my absolute faith that God is in the midst of every single thing, always working to bring life out of death: I would not have these things if my faith of invincibility had held up. If my illusions had continued unpunctured, I would not be awake to the fullness of life.

I am grateful for it all. Even the worst of it is a gift. It is all gift. It is all grace. I lost my life and was made new.

It takes all of it to make me who I am. None of it was wasted, not one minute. None of it could be excised out of me, and leave me still being me. Romans 8:28 says, "All things work together for good for those who love God, who are called according to his purpose." That had previously been a biblical shoulder-patting dismissal of deep pain that had buffered my invincible faith and kept me above or outside of the world. But this translation is inaccurate. The original Greek reads more like, "In all things, *God works for the good, together with those who love God* and are called according to God's purposes."[2] God's purpose is wholeness, fullness, love. God is working in all of my life experiences to contribute to that purpose in me. And God is not just in my life, but in every situation, in every life, everywhere. Instead of separating me from the world, this pushes me *into* the world, to watch there for God's work, and to join in that work together with God for the good.

When we surrender to God's grace that reorients our life, we might do crazy, illogical things, like fall in love with a dying person, or let someone see and love us at our weakest and most vulnerable. Grace impacts us right now. But like a meddling time traveler, grace also alters the past. What was only pain becomes a rich source of strength. What we thought would break us turns out to have broken us open—to love more deeply and widely, to be more fully alive.

All death in my life has been a precursor to resurrection. Going through the death parts, sticking with the discomfort, learning to trust that in Christ, death will not have the final word, I have come out the other side accepting that there is strength in weakness. I'm braver, more willing to be vulnerable, quicker to rest, more open to joy. And I'm absolutely certain that underneath, behind, and through it all, we do belong to God and each other. This is God's world. In all things, God is working for good, and I am along for the ride.

The story God is telling of our lives keeps unfolding and will do so even after we're physically gone from this earth, because God keeps bringing good from all things. The events of our lives happen, and we move on, but the story of our life keeps changing; it is not static and settled. My friend the storyteller Mark Yaconelli says our life experiences don't disappear; they become deep wells we can return to again and again. They show us new things, give us new gifts. Grace quenches us anew in old experiences. Death happens. But then, resurrection. Resurrection is what defines my story. I am grateful.

After the grace-filled, joy-soaked evening celebrating Marty's life, saying the goodbyes and the thank-yous that were on our hearts, people continued to bring Marty meals and pay for housecleaning. They sent cards, made calls, drove with him to appointments, and sat with him in waiting rooms. The frequency of the ER visits increased. The days were harder. The nights became torturous. Sleep was difficult, as tumors impeded bodily functions, and stents or other temporary measures were needed to keep things going. Moments became more frightening, more poignant, more sad, more awake. Still, in the midst of it, Marty persevered, insisting, "I said I would share it with you, and I intend to keep my promise." I answered, "We said we'd walk this road with you, Marty, and we intend to keep our promise too."

Then the day came when he didn't have it in him to leave the house. He didn't need us to remind him of what that meant. He sold his car and paid an extra month's rent and left his house for the last time. With one suitcase, and some assistance, he walked down the stairs and out of his building. He left behind his stunning artisan glass collection to be divvied up between relatives and friends and his driver's license sitting on the kitchen counter with his house keys.

Marty moved into a hospice room that looked like the world's saddest college dorm room. His half of the room was separated from the other side by a wall that didn't quite reach the ceiling. But the nuns were kind, the atmosphere gentle, the bed soft, and the chair easy to get in and out of. And Nancy was there with him. He needed oxygen then. Gone were most of his belongings and most of his independence. His body was wasting away, and his fear had mostly left him. People flooded in to see him for short visits. The visitor log at the front desk was jammed with the names of those who loved Marty.

Whenever I went to visit Marty in hospice, I wore my clerical collar. I went to my wardrobe and pulled out my clergy shirt. Zipping it up behind me, straightening the stiff, white band around my neck, I said aloud, "Why am I doing this?" It wasn't a funeral, and it wasn't a civic engagement. But every time I went to see Marty in hospice, I put it on. It felt right. Did it also feel possibly shallow, or self-serving? Did I want credit for going? Recognition of my role? It was not like the hospice was in a huge hospital setting where it helped to be identified as clergy. It was not like the sisters cared how anyone was dressed or what anyone's role was. *Friends. Family.* So many came to see him. I came too. And each time, I wore my collar. *Pastor.*

One Sunday after church, a few of us drove over to visit Marty. We brought him tart, sparkling lemonade—the only thing that was tasting good to him these days. He dragged his oxygen tank out to the patio, and we sat around a table in the shade, listening to the birds. He seemed fine, if a little tired. We laughed, talked, even sang a couple rounds of "Amazing Grace" to him, since we had a few choir members with us. He smiled in genuine appreciation.

"Marty, it's Pentecost," I told him, and explained,

Today we did something I think you would have liked. We took this month's tithe money, and instead of giving it to a charity or another congregation, we turned it into one hundred dollar bills and put it in envelopes. We drew names and gave seventeen people an envelope with one hundred dollars inside, and the assignment to go out into the world and ask God who they should bless with it. We're calling it our "Pentecost Practice Run"—practicing with something tangible, like cash, to help all of us learn how to do that with our lives every day. In two weeks, people are going to share what they did with the money. Marty, we've got a two-year-old, a visitor from Britain, and all sorts of folks in between who left church today with one hundred dollars and an assignment.

Marty's eyes lit up. "That's wonderful!" he said. "I want to be part of it." He leaned on my arm and dragged his oxygen tank as we left the patio and made our way slowly back to his room. "Hang on a minute," he said. He went over to his small desk, opened the drawer, and took out his checkbook. "Will you give this to Maisy?" he asked. Writing out a check, he tore it off and handed it to me. "Ask her to be my blessing in the world. Ask her to pray and find someone to give this to." My breath caught in my throat, and I felt the tears well up.

"Sure, Marty. I would be happy to," I gulped out. Then we each hugged him and left. We had stayed a half hour—ten minutes too long. Our visit wore him out.

I took the money home and gave it to Maisy. She received the assignment with great reverence. "Really, Mom? He wanted me to do it?" She looked at me with her eyes shining. "I feel so honored."

For more than a week she prayed about whom to give the money to.

Life doesn't give us a blueprint or a timeline in advance. We make our choices, each day, each season. We live our circumstances, waking up each morning and doing that day, and then lying down at night, satisfied or not, to do it all again tomorrow. One day it ends. Our life is summed up, and the verdict is rendered. What will we leave behind us; what will our story have been?

Some people make an obvious impact on the world. Their kindness and goodness shape those around them. Their presence seems to leave a wake, or carve a path for others to follow, for us to emulate—the "great cloud of witnesses." They make the world a better place. When their story is told, it is said that they were a good person. They lived a good life. It is what we all aspire to, perhaps, and secretly wonder if we're getting there.

Tabitha, whose story is told in Acts 9, is one of these people. She is a respected leader, referred to with the title *disciple*—the only feminine use of that noun in the whole Bible. We are given her Aramaic name, Tabitha, which means "grace," and her Greek name as well, Dorcas, which means "gazelle." Giving us both names means she may have been widely known, may have spoken more than one language, perhaps traveled between communities. In any case, Tabitha is deeply treasured and greatly respected, so much so that when she dies, her friends and neighbors send two men to Peter, to ask him to come. He should know she's gone. Really, she's too good a person to let go.

Peter arises and goes. And when he arrives, the room is filled with grieving people. They're holding up tunics and clothing she made for them, displaying tangible proof of her impact and care. It was a big deal to make a piece of clothing in those days, the process was labor intensive. There was even a law that if you borrowed a tunic, you had to return it by sundown, because it might be the only one someone owned. And here the whole room is filled with tunics Tabitha had made. No one could deny that she was a busy, productive, good, and influential person, a benefit to her community, a blessing to the world. Tabitha was a model follower of Jesus. She became a saint, in fact. She is now Saint Tabitha the Widow in the Greek Orthodox Church, and her feast day is October 25. Roman

Catholics commemorate her as Dorcas, and Dorcas Societies, which provide clothing for the poor, are named after her. Protestant churches commemorate her along with Lydia in January. Tabitha was without doubt an exemplary disciple.

But just before Tabitha's story, we are told about another person whom Peter prays for and asks Jesus to heal. The text names this man too: Aeneas. This man is paralyzed. He's been confined to his bed for eight years already and will, presumably, remain there until he is transferred from his bed to his grave. If he is known in his community, it is not for his contributions, but for the burden he is. Everything that he needs, others must help him do. Bathing, dressing, toileting, eating. The labels and identity the world has put on Aeneas lock him into impossibility. His is a life written off. According to the world's definitions, which calculate the worth of a life by capability instead of care, his story went quiet years ago, his possibility quenched. Any chance Aeneas had of living a good life, making an impact on the world, being productive, and contributing things of value is long over. By the measure of the way of fear, he's already dead.

Death is the absence of life. Tabitha has died. Her life is over. The ink is dry, the hourglass empty. In effect, Aeneas has too. He is living in death, waiting for death.

And then the word, a command that interrupts both of their deaths with life: *Anesthi! Arise!*

The name of the hospital ship I spent six months on in West Africa after I graduated from college was the *Anastasis*, which is Greek for "resurrection." Children, women, and men with tumors, twisted limbs, or cleft palates were brought aboard. These were people outcast in their society. They were barred from full participation by the identities and prejudices the world had projected on them. They were laid down in the hospital wing and put under for surgery, and when they awoke, when they arose, they had moved from death to life. A new life opened before them, a life with hope and possibility that had been dead to them before. God interrupted their story with a different story, and their lives became a witness to the love of God, a window to God's grace.

"Get up!" Peter tells Aeneas. *Anesthi!* Arise! "Get up and make your bed." What use would he have had for a made bed if he was always in it? Now he is leaving it, so Peter says, *Make your bed*, you're going into the world. *Instead of a bed for sickness, Aeneas, make yourself a bed for rest. Move from death into new life, Aeneas.*

Immediately Aeneas gets up, and his arising becomes the story that turns the hearts of all those in the region to Jesus. His rising witnesses to God's love, gives them a window to God's grace. It changes his identity in their eyes: Aeneas, the man God healed; Aeneas, the risen one. His true identity all along is now on display for the others to see: *Beloved, Child of God, one for whom God acts.*

Back to Tabitha of the tunics. She mattered so much to so many. If value is measured and identity defined by our productivity and contribution, Tabitha's life was valuable. She was a good and faithful disciple of our Lord Jesus Christ. The evidence of her goodness, her faithfulness, her worth, was all around her in her death, on display in the very room. *See how good she was? See what an impact she made?*

But before Peter prays for her, he banishes all of that from the room. All the people and the tunics and the grief, all the stories of her faithfulness, the symbols of her value, and the signs of her impact. Now Peter kneels down and prays. Then he turns to the body and says, *Get up. Anesthi! Arise!*

Tabitha opens her eyes and sees Peter. She sits up. He reaches out his hand and helps her get up. Calling back in all the people, he presents her to them—alive. And just like the last, this story spreads and turns people to Jesus, a witness to God's love, a window to God's grace.

The Christian story celebrates a good life lived. We should all aspire to a life like Tabitha's. We should help each other be disciples. But Tabitha is not resurrected because she has lived a good life. Tabitha is resurrected and given life because Jesus is the resurrection and the life. She is defined now as *Beloved, Child of God, one for whom God acted.*

Aeneas has no value that society could affirm; he makes no impact. He is no model disciple or productive contributor. He's certainly not changing the world. In the world's eyes, his life is already over. In the way of fear, Aeneas has no worth. And yet God resurrects him too. Tabitha is trying to live a good life inside the story of Jesus Christ. But the story of Jesus Christ is so big that it even comes to those who don't live what the world considers to be a good life.

So immersed as we are in the way of fear, so caught in comparing and competing, in measuring our worth and earning our place, we might be tempted to believe Tabitha has earned the right to resurrection. But that's not how the way of God works. God's resurrection is so generous and promiscuous that it comes also to the ones who can't possibly earn a thing. And even though she is a model disciple whom we should strive to emulate, even so, Tabitha too needs God to act for her.

When Aeneas dies, the townspeople won't hold up what he accomplished. They will hold up what God did for him. And the same is now true of Tabitha. She is no longer defined by what she has accomplished. That died with her first death. Now she too is defined by what God has done for her. Both stories are interrupted with resurrection. Rise up, get up, and live. *Anesthi!*

I'm willing to bet that most of us want to live in a way that when we die, they will tell stories and hold up examples and symbols of what a good life we've lived. But even when circumstances make it impossible to live the kind of life that would earn us such affirmation, God's act reaches us, comes to us, and gives us new life. Because that is who God is. That is what God does. Tabitha and Aeneas share dignity, inherent worthiness, and wholeness in the eyes of God. Neither Tabitha's death nor Aeneas's healing alters those fundamentals. That they are already beloved, children of God, is true of them before and despite anything they did or didn't, could or couldn't, do with their lives. This is true of us as well. The things that we think limit us or keep us from fullness of life are not what define us. The ways we measure our worth and value turn out to be flimsy and false. And into our places of death, resurrection comes.

Before anything even happens, this story is already subversive; the gospel always flips the cultural script. The one who has lived a good life, the respected leader and true disciple, is a woman. This woman has done so much for everyone. The one who can't do anything for himself is a man. He has no good acts to commend him; for eight years he's been seen as nothing but his need. And the story of Jesus's incarnation, crucifixion, and resurrection gets played out equally in both their lives.

In the name of Jesus Christ, to the paralyzed man, Peter says, *Arise! Get up! Anesthi!* To the dead woman, in Jesus's name, Peter says, *Arise! Get up! Anesthi!* And both of them do. They both become part of the story of the church, shared and treasured, alongside each other. (Because it is Peter through whom they are healed—the one of whom Jesus said, "Upon this rock I will build my church" [Matt 16:18]—the foundations of Saint Peter's in Rome are built on their stories.)

The resurrection of Jesus changes everything. Death does not get to have the last word. Not when death comes to us as suffering, or injury, or loss of mind or mobility, or the end of a dream or plan, and not when it comes to us as a life ended, our accomplishments on display amid our weeping loved ones.

One of my favorite parts of being a pastor is doing funerals. In our tradition, we don't officially call it a funeral, a memorial service, or a celebration of life. We call it "a service of witness to the resurrection." And all the loved ones who want to tell stories of their person, how good they were, what an impact they had—their storytelling is fine and lovely. Seeing someone's life defined by discipleship or charity, marked by goodness and kindness, is inspiring. Celebrating a life well lived is beautiful and important.

But even for those who've lived an exemplary, good life, that's not the totality of who they are. Inside all of our stories is the darkness too. The pain we've caused, the pain we hide. The failures and struggles we've never overcome. Sometimes at funerals I feel as though we hold up an invisible scale, into which we feel the need to pile up the praiseworthy good on one side against the unspoken bad on the other, hoping it tips enough in the right direction for our loved one's life to be considered worthy. But what about the life cut short? The life misdirected? What about the secret sins we hide, the failures we fear ever letting out into the light in case they cement us in our unworthiness?

No matter what our story, when our loved ones gather at our funeral, the final word spoken over us witnesses not to the goodness or worthiness of our lives, but to the resurrection of our Lord. That each of our lives, in myriad ways, reveals the grace of God that comes to us in death and brings new life. That each of us is a unique window into the story of the Divine, who joins us and redeems us and connects us in love to God and each other.

No matter how worthy or worthless, well lived or wasted, impressive or depressing, productive or paralyzed a life may be, and no matter what proof there is of goodness or lack of opportunity to try, each life is a witness to the love and grace of God.

None of us knows our trajectory or our end, really. We get the chance to live as good a life as we can. And we should help each other do that. But we should also know this: we will not be measured by how well or poorly we accomplished that.

When this life is over, we will be mourned and missed, and we will be embraced and welcomed by the God who took on all sin and death so that nothing might ever separate us from the love of God in Christ Jesus. Our value is already declared by the God who claims the world in love and names each one of us, *Beloved, Child of God*. Everything else is the canvas on which that story is painted, the paper on which that portrait is written. Ultimately, what tells the story of our life is grace.

Chapter 12

When We Live
Now What Will Be

———

The worst isn't the last thing about the world.
It's the next to the last thing. The last thing is
the best. It's the power from on high that comes
down into the world, that wells up from the
rock-bottom worst of the world like a hidden
spring. Can you believe it? The last, best thing
is the laughing deep in the hearts of the saints,
sometimes our hearts even. Yes. You are terribly loved and forgiven. Yes. You are healed. All
is well.

—FREDERICK BUECHNER, *The Final Beast*

The end is the meaning of all. And the mode in
which it is present is hope. . . . Hope integrates.

It makes whole. . . . Hope is the passion for the possible.

—BR. DAVID STEINDL-RAST,
Gratefulness, the Heart of Prayer

June 2017

A week after Pentecost I receive a call from Marty's brother, David. Marty has taken a turn. They are guessing he has less than a week left. When I walk into Marty's room, I see a different man from a week earlier. He is frail, the sheet pulled up to his chin, his eyes closed. The flesh has fallen away from his face. His legs are swollen and heavy, feet sticking out the bottom of the covers, taut and puffy. He is asleep.

Nancy rises from the chair to hug me. She thanks me for coming, and we slip out of his room to talk. "He's in and out," she tells me.

"How are you doing?" I ask her.

"I'm surprisingly OK," she answers.

When we return, I sit beside Marty, taking his hand in mine.

"Hi, Marty," I whisper. "I brought communion." He struggles to wake up.

"Marty," Nancy says, leaning over him, sweeping the hair off his forehead. "Kara's here. Can you wake up?" He moves around, eyes opening and closing again. "She brought you communion, Marty. Would you like to take it?"

Marty forces his eyes open and struggles to sit. Nancy pushes the button to lift the head of his bed. She sits down on a chair opposite me, each of us taking one of his hands. Marty looks at me.

"Hi, Kara," he says. Then he drifts back to sleep.

She wakes him again, and I speak the words of institution. I tell him this is Jesus's body, broken for us and our broken bodies, which one day will be made whole. I tell him we eat on this side of eternity to connect us to the day when we will be fully, wholly alive with Christ.

And then I pick up the small wafer and hold it out to him. He tries to lift his hand to take it from me but can't. I place it on his lips, but he can't take it into his mouth. He can barely keep his eyes open. I take it off of his mouth and set it on the tray next to his dinner—a half peanut butter sandwich—and place the tiny cup of grape juice next to it. "You can take this with dinner, Marty," I say.

And then I hand a wafer to Nancy, and she and I eat and drink, our eyes meeting over him while he lies still between us. I whisper a prayer, kiss his forehead, and leave.

When I get into my car, I sit in the parking lot and cry. He is so much worse than I'd expected. He is slipping away.

The next evening I return. Again, I put on my clerical shirt. This feels almost like a ceremony. I'm mystified as to why, and questioning my own motives, but nevertheless, I zip myself into it before heading out of the house. This time I bring with me Lisa, our parish associate, part of Marty's care team, and a steady support to his sister, Susan.

"He's not speaking," Nancy says when we enter the room. The lights are dim, and the sun is setting outside the window. It feels peaceful. He isn't asleep, but he isn't really awake either. I open the Bible and begin to read some lines from Psalms:

> I lift my eyes to the hills; where does my help come
>   from?
> Oh, Lord, you have searched me and known me. . . .
> The Lord is my shepherd. . . .

He moans a few times. Lisa holds his hand.
We sing his favorite song:

> Open our eyes, Lord,
> we want to see Jesus . . .

We pray again. It feels like church. We say goodbye.

The next evening, I send a message to the congregation. "I am reading psalms with Marty at seven thirty. Anyone who wishes to be there is welcome." Sue, the elder who had met my eyes across the room on the day of Marty's commissioning service, who headed up his care team and took him for late-night ER runs, texts back, "I'll be there."

It feels different this night. He looks different. Gaunter. Paler. The lighting is bright. A new roommate is just moving in on the other side of the divider. We can't see them, but we hear conversation and questions and have the sense that they are aware of us, listening, even as we are aware of them.

Marty is restless. It feels stilted. I read the same psalms as last night, but there's no peace. He keeps reaching out, grabbing me and pulling me close. Grabbing Sue, leaning into her face, urgently, as though he has something to say, to ask. But no words come. He is there but not. He is agitated. It is hard seeing him this way.

I say goodbye to Sue in the parking lot. It seems like years ago that we were sitting on the patio drinking sparkling lemonade.

We are made of the stuff of dust—the stuff of stars, but the stuff of dust too. We are not invincible, and not unlimited; each of us comes with an expiration date. Human beings are finite, dependent creatures, bound to this earth, to each other, and to our Maker. And this is grace. We need God.

So God ministers to us. God provides for us. God loves and cares for us, and we are designed to receive God's love and care. We're made to be loved. To trust our Source. To know our place alongside others. To care for the other creatures we are so bound to on this earth-home we can't escape. To live on it and in it. And from inside our own creatureliness, we are made to speak and listen to God.

But we can't do this alone. We are not solo, individual creatures. (For just a short time God tried this out, and it didn't work.) To be made in the image of a relational God, whose love in Father, Son, and Spirit spilled out into creation to be shared and spread, humans need also to be in relationship. We need also to belong to other than just ourselves, and even other than just God. Once there is an other, a you, there is now also a self, a me, and now the image of God can be reflected in a relationship of dialogue, the mutual vulnerability of knowing and being known, a conversation, a community. Now there is belonging. Belonging to God is complete even as we belong to each other. Belonging to each other is part of our belonging to God. This is *hesed*, and this is grace.

But how risky and weak it feels to be bound by the constraints of time and space, life and death, bodies and needs! Oh, to be invincible! So we humans try to be more than we are. This is our sin. We strain to transcend our limits. And we're pretty good at it, or at least we feel like we are. We can know what is happening at every moment in every corner of the earth, and we can extend our reach to digitally become enemies with those we don't know and friends with those we've never met. We keep the lights on and the screens lit to work around the clock, always available and always responsive. We eat everything we feel like and drink till we stop feeling. We hold in front of ourselves false images of fake bodies and then contort ourselves around diets and drugs and gurus and equipment to become something we are not. We ignore our responsibility for the earth and its creatures, pursuing our own invincibility instead. We allow some people to prosper on the deprivation of other people, propping up ideologies and practices that dehumanize, degrade, and divide. We resent and punish other human beings for their weakness or need. We see vulnerability as a deficit, a danger.

We, in so very many ways, suppress our humanity, disregard our interdependence, and deny our need for a minister, for others to care for us. We choose alienation. We become disconnected. We hide. We hide from ourselves, from others, and most futilely, we try to hide from God. We disintegrate. We lose our very selves, our primary identity and belonging.

On that day back in 2009 when our journey together as a church was just getting started and I went on retreat to the Franciscan nuns' retreat center with Wayne Muller's *Sabbath* book tucked in my bag, I came up from my cozy yurt to the big farmhouse kitchen and sat at the lunch table with three sisters and the mother superior. Somehow the conversation came around to the fact that monastic communities were facing the same struggles churches were facing: a deficit of young people, a generation not as interested in religion, an institution dying.

"There are very few young women signing up to be nuns these days," she said. But she showed no anxiety or concern about this. Quite the opposite, in fact. She leaned across the table to me and, with eyes twinkling, said, "You know, if you and I are the ones who turn off the lights and lock the doors behind us, God isn't finished. It's just time for something else."

She leaned back and continued, "Monastic communities, since their inception, have held on to something valuable on behalf of the rest of culture, something that culture has forgotten. In the fourteenth century, it was the Scriptures. Monks painstakingly copied them by hand so they wouldn't be lost. But then came the printing press, and suddenly, no more need for that. Did that mean God was finished? Of course not!"

She paused and smiled, and then said, "The thing that we are now hanging on to on behalf of the rest of culture is *Sabbath*."

I think about that day a lot. It was formative in our Sabbath journey. The choice to stop on purpose and let God meet us made space for all we experienced together in the next decade. It made us open to God and one another in profound ways. But now I wonder if there wasn't also another message there for us.

Just like monastic communities and their particular calling to hold on to something the rest of the culture has forgotten, I wonder if we who find ourselves in the church, showing up in little congregations here and there, don't have a similar calling. Even as the institutional church as we've known it in America, with all its power, influence, structure, and voice, is coming to an end, I wonder if we don't have a very clear purpose in the midst of all this. Perhaps we too are called to hold on to something that most of the culture around us forgets most of the time. I wonder if it isn't our job to hold on to our humanity, our most fundamental, essential identity: our belongingness to God and one another.

As the church in America seems to be dying, the church at large, the body of Christ in the world, has a further horizon and a life that will not die. The church is the people whose right-now lives are shaped by the very, very end. We have a further horizon than the next exciting innovation or the next interesting cultural trend. We live from the future that is coming. We live from the time when all that remains will be the love and belongingness of God. Christ came into this time when all will die to bring us into the time when all will live. So now our life is guided not by what is but by what will be. We are those who premember the future of God.

We dream of this future, and speak of it, and sing about it, and trust in it. And sometimes, I'm sure, we sound ridiculous as we talk about peace or justice or courage or kindness in the midst of a violent, unjust, cruel, and fearful world. But we do it because we know what is coming. We live out of peace and justice and courage in the face of, in contrast to, the utter absence of such things. We bear the tension of knowing what's coming even while what is in front of us is *not that.* So we live not from what is, but from what will be. We might call this vision "eschatological imagination."

We trust that the end of things is not humans bailing off this misused earth to a happy place in the sky or a burning place underground, never to return. And the end isn't about God giving up on this cosmic failed project, wiping the slate clean, and starting fresh. The end of things is a new beginning for all things.

For God who made, and claimed, and came into this world to give up on this world or any of us in it is utterly incongruent. That will never happen, ever. This whole big wonderful and broken world belongs to God. Nobody loves all of this as God does. And God will never abandon it. God will never abandon any of us.

So when God says, "See, I am making all things new" (Rev 21:5), we have confidence that this is true. Indeed, God is making you, me, this tired earth and its broken creatures, this messed-up, beloved, and confused church, and all of creation new. And like the Creator who walked the garden in the cool of the evening, and the Word that became flesh and dwelled among us, God will come, and God's forever home will be here, where God's heart is. With God's people, in God's crea-tion. And when that happens, "death will be no more; mourn-ing and crying and pain will be no more" (Rev 21:4).

The very, very end will be both the righting of all wrong and deep, unparalleled intimacy between God and humanity, God and creation, each of us and all of us, our belonging to each other as we are meant to, all life in harmony. This is the church's heart song. We sing this not for ourselves but for the whole world. Our congregation has been learning to sing this song through *worship*, *hospitality*, and *Sabbath*.

We show up alongside each other to praise God and wait for God to meet us, because of what will be and so already is. The day is coming when God will be so close to us that we will delight in God's presence and God will delight in us. So through *worship* we practice for that day. We prepare and anticipate and live into that day right now.

We seek to be with and for others, making space for each other's joy and sharing each other's suffering, because of what will be and so already is. The day is coming when there will be no more weeping or despair or sadness, only connection and belonging and fulfillment. So through *hospitality*, we practice for that day. We prepare and anticipate and live into that day right now.

And we seek to pause and notice and be consciously present in our lives, where God is already waiting to meet us. We stop and step out of the relentless pull to produce and consume because resting reminds us of what will be and so already is. The day is coming when all striving, comparing, and competing will cease, and we will live forever in the fullness of life and joy. So through *Sabbath* we practice for that day. We prepare and anticipate and live into that day right now.

Because our faith is eschatological (shaped by what will be), it is never complete; it is always becoming. Like the father in Mark who says, "I believe; help my unbelief!" (Mark 9:24), our faith is real only when it is up against our doubts, our hope only exists up against despair. We name our unbelief even as we believe; we share our despair from our yearning for the hope that is promised. We trust in God's fullness of life up against our nothingness.

The church is the people of this faith, the community of this hope. We don't *bring* the new reality; we trust that *God is bringing it.* God is always already at work; we help each other notice what God is doing. We practice justice, love belonging-ness, and walk humbly with our God (Mic 6:8) in order to join in what God is already doing.

We are people of a dead and resurrected Lord. We don't back down from nothingness; we don't hide from death. We claim that death is not the end that it appears to be, and it is certainly not the last word. Church is those who walk right into death expecting to find life, because that is where God is and that is what God does.

Friday morning, I text Nancy. "How was the night?" I ask.

"Rough," she texts back. "Can you come over? They think it will be soon."

I am in the drive-through lane of a coffee shop, a block away from our church building, when I get the message. I am on my way to lead a prayer service, then a meeting. I call someone who is planning to be at both and ask her to take over. I text the others and tell them where I will be.

And then as I drive, I debate. Should I go right there? That seems the right thing to do. But I want to stop at home and put on my collar first. *Why? Why does it matter? Isn't it important that I just go? What if I miss him because my vanity, or insecurity, gets in the way?* And then, without having a clear reason to do so, I go home and put on the collar.

When I arrive, Marty is pale, shrunken, halfway gone. His breathing is shallow and irregular. Nancy is there, his sister, Susan, arrives, his oldest friend, Brian, joins us. We sit all around Marty, two of us on each side. I anoint him once more and pray a blessing. The atmosphere feels still and suspended. We talk in hushed voices. We hold his hand, all of us together, all the hands surrounding and enfolding his, like the arms that rested on his body in his commissioning service. We tell him we love him.

And then I sense that work is done. It is finished. We sit in silence for a beat or two, and then we begin to say a few things to each other. Some memories about Marty, mixed with some talk about the weather, or the drive over, perhaps. Across him, around him, a brief conversation by the living. After a few minutes, we turn our attention back to Marty. And we realize that he is gone.

Chapter 13

When We Live with and for Each Other, God Meets Us

———◆———

I am
A hole in a flute
That the Christ's breath moves through—
Listen to this
Music.

—HAFIZ, *The Gift*

Resurrection is not revival, survival, resuscitation.
Resurrection is not a coming back to this life of
    death.
What would be the point of that?
Resurrection is a going forward into death
and through death
into a fullness that is beyond life and death as we
    know them.
From this side of the great divide,

death remains all we can see. . . .
Hope looks squarely at death, the open door for
    Surprise.

        —BR. DAVID STEINDL-RAST,
Gratefulness, the Heart of Prayer (formatting mine)

A few days after Marty's death, on a sunny June afternoon, I stand in front of two hundred people gathered
in the church sanctuary. Atheists and pagans, a small Wiccan
contingent, astrologers and health administrators, friends
from Hutchinson and friends from the bar, lifelong Presbyterians and cradle Catholics, a dozen people who had known
Marty for more than fifty years, and another dozen who had
known him only a couple of months but whose lives had been
changed by him and so they wanted to pay respects: all are
gathered here together. I look out at the beautiful hodgepodge of humanity, the congregation Marty assembled and
entrusted to me to minister to in this moment. And this is
what I say:

> Marty would say, "You can never have too many
> friends." And I imagine his life like a high school
> cafeteria—each table a different group. His church
> friends, his bar friends, his Hutch friends, his astrol-
> ogy friends, his Gunflint Trail friends, his *old* friends.
> And Marty, with his lunch tray, effortlessly flowing
> between them, a full part of each group. His super-
> power in this life was friendship. And now here we
> all are, sitting at one big table—in a room together
> with people whose paths might never have any other

reason to cross, except that in some way we all belonged to Marty, and he to us. I find that utterly enchanting.

I believe that Marty has returned to his source, to love, to the force that made him and gave him his insatiable love for people, his boundless passion for the outdoors, his drive to get as much as he could out of life and give as much as he could to life. There is nothing hidden in him that isn't revealed, nothing brokenhearted in him that isn't healed, no pain that he carried or caused in this life that is not released, nothing holding him back in any way from full and complete love. Marty now rests his whole being in the being that called his being into being. And that is comforting for me to envision.

"Alone and afraid." Those were the two words Marty used when he learned his cancer wasn't responding to treatment and it would likely take him. It's the part he dreaded, the part that scared him the most: he felt alone, and he felt afraid. He prayed that he wouldn't feel alone or afraid. But those are also the two words I heard used in reference to the day he left this earth: "When Marty died, he wasn't alone, and he wasn't afraid." And while I believe God answered his prayer, I have to hand it to Marty for making God's job easy on that front, because Marty let us in. He let us share it with him. He let us be there for him.

We believe around here that in Jesus, God came to take on everything inside us, between us, and thrust upon us by the world that makes us feel alone and afraid. That the cross means God bears all suffering alongside, with, and for us. And because of that, when we are alongside, with, and for each other, bearing one another's suffering, we meet God. Marty let us do that alongside, with, and for him. And Marty did not hesitate to be alongside, with, and for others. This is a holy, human, sacred thing. It's where God is. And when we do this we are not alone, and we are not afraid.

I loved being Marty's pastor. I learned so much from him these past eighteen months. He would come to me anxious and ask, "Do people really want to hear how bad it's getting? I don't want to be a burden." And I would remind him that he promised to share it all with us. I would tell him that if he made it look too easy, he was "false advertising for the rest of us." And I would say again what a blessing his honesty—in the whole struggle of it all—was to us. And it was true. He changed this community. He showed us how to be open and real even in the things you don't choose and are not glad about. He gave us a chance to live out with him another of his life mottoes—we are here to take care of each other.

And I would sit with him in a kind of wonder as he would share about a lunch with friends, his face open with delight and joy, eyes sparkling and smile wide. And then a wave of grief would come, and he would sob with deep, heartrending sorrow at having to leave this life. And after a few minutes, the tears would subside, his shoulders would lift, and a new story would come, one of gratitude, or hope, or wondering what dying would be like and what would happen to him beyond. And sometimes fear would surface, and he'd talk through the flashes of terror or apprehension until that departed and the next emotion arose.

And in these times, I felt like, for Marty, the layers we all live with, that insulate us from the raw reality of living, had been stripped away, and he was awake for it all. Noticing so deeply, appreciating so profoundly, grieving so honestly, celebrating so freely. In these conversations, he would let anger, sadness, joy, gratitude, and hope move through him without resisting, hiding, or censoring. He was done with games. He just wanted to live every moment of his one precious life to its fullest. And he did.

We've heard a lot today about what a great guy Marty was and how much dignity he died with. And that was all true. And there might be the feeling that somehow to do him honor we shouldn't feel sad. We should celebrate his life. We should be glad he's no longer suffering. We should avoid the small anger pressing at the base of the skull, the sorrow that claws up the back of the throat. Swallow it down and just try to be thankful for the beauty of his life and the peacefulness of his death.

I am going to tell you not to do that. I am going to tell you that the anger is a gift, and the sorrow and grief are a treasure. Because they point to the deeper longing for things that are wrong to be right. They point to how beloved he was and how much he loved living. They bring us to that place where God is alongside, with, and for us. And I will not downplay any of that. It's too important to skip over.

Marty was taken too soon. That's just a fact. Most of us are, and we can deal with each of those stories when our own turn comes, but I want to talk for a minute about what makes me angry about Marty's death. Marty should have had a chance to enjoy his retirement. He was *so* looking forward to it—oh, the plans he had! Marty should have had a chance to turn more of us into *old* friends and make more new ones to add to his collection. He should have gone to England; he should have traveled and experienced more of this earth he so loved. He should have taken on new hobbies and interests; he so loved diving into something new and exploring it completely. He should have married Nancy and been a grandpa. He should have grown old along with someone; he told me he always wanted that. Marty had dreams and longings and hopes that never got to be fulfilled.

And that makes me angry. It makes me sad. I wanted those things for him too. I wanted to be there alongside, with, and for him in those things, and see him be alongside, with, and for others in the things we all have ahead of us—the new sister or brother arriving in our congregation soon, this generation of kids he's watched start to grow up, graduating from school and heading out into the world. All the joyous and heartbreaking things that are coming in all the lives of those gathered in this room that Marty would have celebrated and grieved alongside, with, and for each of us. I will wail for the loss of that. When the feelings come, I will let them come.

And only then, only once those feelings pass through and space is made for the next ones, will I turn to the gratitude. Oh! What an incomparable honor to have known and been a part of Marty's life! To have walked on this earth alongside his soul, to have shared this breathtakingly beautiful planet, filled with a never-ending diversity of interesting people, spectacular views, new challenges, old stories, winding trails and pounding waterfalls and crisp forest air, and lapping lakes at sunset. To be in this life, every single day—to be alive! This is a blessing beyond compare! And to share it with others! What purpose! What privilege!

We are told that "neither death, nor life, nor angels, nor rulers, nor things present, nor things to come, nor powers, nor height, nor depth, nor anything else in all creation, will be able to separate us from the love of God in Christ Jesus our Lord" (Rom 8:38). We are told that all that separates us from love and wholeness, makes us feel alone or afraid, or keeps us from what should have been is borne into the very heart of God. None of it is forgotten, overlooked, moved past. It is treasured, precious, and sacred, the sorrow and the loss, held with tender care by the Love that will not end. And one day all wrongs will be made right.

Marty's being rests in that love now, and all that he just poked a finger into, just dipped a toe in, just scratched the surface of, he now knows and feels fully and completely, just as he is fully and completely known (1 Cor 13:12). Marty is part of our cloud of witnesses, those who've gone before us whose lives have been tangled up in ours and, just by being human beings next to us, point us now and then to what's really real.

Marty loved rituals that opened us to God and connected us to timelessness and the cosmos and each other, so here is how we're going to finish this service and honor Marty together. First, alongside, with, and for each other now, in both our gratitude and our loss, we are going to recite a poem written by another person who believed "life is meant to be lived outdoors," a few thousand years ago, a shepherd turned king, Psalm 23. We will say the words shared by people in all circumstances for millennia, words that were also read by a few of us with Marty on his last couple of evenings before he left us, and left all these scattered groups of friends to gather here as one.

And after that, we are going to sing Marty's favorite song, a song that expressed how Marty chose to live his life, "What a Wonderful World," and we will let it witness to us, like his life did, a giant thank-you. Thank you for it all.

And then this is what we do. We recite the psalm together, and we sing the song together, and then we leave. And the pagans bring a living butterfly with them from the sanctuary, where it has been quietly flitting about in a fabric cage on the floor near a pew throughout the service, and we all gather on the patio and watch them release it. It flies into the air and disappears over the top of the tall oak tree into the sunlight. Then one of them turns to me and says, "For us, a butterfly is a sign of new life, a symbol of resurrection."

"It's that for us too," I answer, smiling.

Marty died on a Friday. On Saturday Maisy said to me, "Mom, I think when I keep praying about who to give the money to, I am not getting an answer because I already know. I think I have known all along." She told me she wanted to give it to the homeless man who stood with a sign on the exit ramp on the way to church. For years he had been on her radar. She regularly anticipated seeing him on Sunday mornings on the way to church. She made sure we kept the car stocked with hand warmers in the winter and granola bars in the summer so she could reach out the window and give him something as we waited at the light to turn the corner. This is whom she wanted to give the money to.

"OK, Maisy. But you need to know this connects us now. We all belong to each other. It's not just giving money to a stranger; you are practicing this belonging. So now you commit to praying for him too, and we watch for other ways God is asking us to be with and for him, OK?"

"OK, Mom," she answered.

She cashed Marty's check and put the money into an envelope she decorated with hearts and flowers and smiling faces. We prayed that the man would be there when we drove by the next day.

On Sunday, we pulled onto the exit ramp. "He's here!" Maisy exclaimed.

Andy brought the car to a stop at the curb, and Maisy and I got out and crossed the street, holding hands. When we got to the other side, we approached the man. He was sitting on an overturned bucket, a cardboard sign in one hand and a cane in the other.

He was a stranger. I couldn't begin to understand what his life was like. And yet he was a human being whose life was just like my own. The barriers between us were not the real reality; the real reality was our belonging to God and one another.

"Hello. I'm Maisy," she said to him. "This is my mom, Kara."

"Hi, Maisy and Kara; I'm David," he answered.

Maisy cleared her throat and plunged in. "My friend Marty gave me this money and asked me to pray about who to give it to. I did, and I chose to give it to you."

She held out the envelope to him. "He died on Friday," she added.

"Oh!" David said. His weathered face filled with compassion. "I am so sorry about your friend." And he reached out to Maisy and hugged her.

"Thank you," he added, taking the envelope from her outstretched hand.

Maisy nodded and smiled shyly. She looked up at me and took my hand again.

"Goodbye, David, have a good day!" she waved.

"Goodbye, Maisy, you too!" he answered, smiling back.

Maisy bounced back to the car and climbed in. We drove the rest of the way to church, and when the time came in worship, she slid out of her pew, stood at the pulpit, and said, "When we did the Pentecost Practice Run, my name was not drawn. But Marty heard about it, and he gave me one hundred dollars so that he could be part of it too. That really meant a lot to me." Then she shared what had just happened on the way in to church that day. She told them about David.

I watched the congregation receive her, this child they'd known since before she could walk, now standing before them proclaiming the gospel at work in her own life. I saw the invisible web that holds us all in the belonging of God, linking us to Marty, who had just left us, and to David, who had just been joined to us through him and through Maisy, by the grace of God.

We lit a candle for Marty. We lit a candle for David. *God in your loving mercy*, we sang, *hear our prayer.*

"I feel sad," I say, "but I am not really grieving. It feels different." I am sitting with my spiritual director, reflecting on the events of the week. "Marty wasn't my *friend*. I was his *pastor*."

This is a space I've only just discovered I occupy. I am a bit in awe as I probe the corners of it, feel around inside myself for what this is. This sense of gratitude, strength, trust, ease. I sat by his bedside as he slipped from this earth, and I had a place there. It was a given that I should be there. *Not family. Not friend. Not loved one*, I think, with awe. *Pastor.* I was Marty's pastor.

"I realize now why I wore the collar," I tell her. "It was like a military uniform. I was honoring Marty and this difficult passage he was navigating. This holy and horrible thing it was to be stepping out of this life one little bit at a time until you are all gone. My collar was a form of salute. I wore it representing 'the faith'; I was there as a stand-in for the church. Wearing the uniform of pastor was like me standing in recognition, hand on heart, to hold sacred Marty's journey. I was his pastor. He needed me to be that. He made me that."

By wearing the collar, I was bearing witness as one ennobled to speak of the afterlife. I was accepting my duty with the solemnity of one expected to do the things that usher us beyond the veil—anointing, prayer, reading Scripture.

"Anyone can do these things," I say, "but nobody does. I do. I did. I came in my clerical shirt, with my Bible and my courage, and I held open the space for tears, for questions, for wondering about the meaning of breath, and moment, and eternity, and sorrow, and goodbye. My presence let people feel safe, somehow, to say out loud their thoughts and fears, their imaginings about what he was going through. It gave them structure, something to lean into when they needed it. *She's going to read a psalm. And then she will pray.*"

I shift in my seat and pause. "And I think it told Marty that each of these stages he was living through was important. Part of it all. Not disconnected. It brought continuity to his spiritual journey. I walked with him to the end. I marked the sign on him that was made at his beginning, when he was baptized as an infant by another pastor who first said the words I last said: *Beloved. Child of God, now and forever.*"

Nancy told me later that she thought I was closer to Marty than anyone else. That wasn't true. I didn't share life with Marty. I didn't hold him in the dark, dreaming about a future, as she did. I didn't share vacations and school memories, inside jokes and life-changing experiences with him as his friend Brian did. I was not part of any of Marty's many cohorts of friends who walked with him in the light-dappled woods; dived with him in the deep, cold sea; or traveled with him in the great, wide world. But I knew what she meant. She meant I was his pastor.

People tell pastors things they don't tell other people. Everyone else mostly saw his dignity, his positivity, his buoyancy in the face of adversity. He showed me his fear. Marty came to me when he needed to break down and cry. When he needed to feel weak. When he had questions the universe couldn't answer. He trusted me to be for him just what he needed a pastor to be. And he showed me how to do it through his trust in me. Because he saw me that way; that is what I was.

God is first minister. It is how God relates to us, by coming alongside us and caring for our real selves in our real circumstances. God enters into our experiences and bears them with us in order to heal us, to bring us to peace and joy, to return us to our true identity as beloved. We live into that identity, into our fullness of life, when we take our place alongside one another as ministers, made in the image of the Divine minister.

To be a pastor is to hold space for Divine encounter. As pastor, I was the one who remembered that we are all ministers and that it is God who does the ministry. We watch together for what God is doing and join in. Christ is present to us, and the Holy Spirit works through us, when we come alongside each other in suffering and joy. I was the one who reminded us of our shared calling and that we minister from our weakness, not our strength. Marty's trust in me helped me trust God, and trust the community, and trust him.

In our polity (church order and structure), we don't believe ordination is a fundamental change in being. It doesn't make the ordained person more holy, more special, or different in any way from other human beings. All it says is that while we are all called to be ministers, a pastor's specific calling is to minister in and for the church, through preaching the Word and administering the sacraments. Other traditions see this differently, but this is how Presbyterians view ordination, and it resonates deeply with what I know to be true of God and community. I am ordained to a role, not to a status. The authority I have is not somehow bestowed from on high directly from God, or even passed down from higher authority within the church. It comes from the community I serve, which recognizes my calling and says yes to it: *Yes, we will accept your leadership and guidance as your form of ministry among us. We will trust you to help us be ministers.*

I was Marty's pastor because Marty welcomed me to be his pastor. I was given the task, by Marty, the congregation, and so by God too, of entrusting them with each other, with Marty, with our shared calling. Jesus said many times, "I am in the Father and the Father is in me and you are in me" (John 14:20; 17:10–11, 21). It's like this: all entwined and interwoven, the dance of shared ministry given breath and life by the Spirit of God.

To be Marty's pastor meant I got to hold space for Marty's humanity as he ministered to us from his weakness. I got to help him accept the ministry of those alongside him, who were also ministering from their weakness. I was his pastor, only in my own weakness, because Marty made me his pastor.

And when it was all over, Marty made me pastor for his friends. "Kara knows what I want for my funeral," he told his sister and brother. To me, he said, "You know what I want for my funeral." And I did. He wanted me to welcome his friends and hold space for their humanity. He wanted the sanctuary to be big enough to hold it all—their weakness and their sorrow too. And he wanted me to remind them of the bigger picture, the deeper love, the wider, wonderful world, and he trusted that when I did, God would meet us. Because of him, I got to be pastor to them all so that they all could minister to each other, and we all could experience the presence of God.

Right now, God is here. Maybe not the God we thought God was, or even, perhaps, the God we wish God were, but the real

God. And God is inviting us to be here too, with God and each other, in our real lives.

That's it. That's why we are here. As Marty would say, we're here to take care of each other. We are each born *Beloved, Child of God*, and we each die *Beloved, Child of God* still, always. And in between, we journey together, connected inextricably. Our humanity, at its core, is this: we all belong to God, and we all belong to each other. This is our primary identity, our ongoing purpose, and our ultimate destination. This is the deepest belonging.

Notes

Chapter 1

1 Sarah Eekhoff Zylstra, "The 8 People Americans Trust More Than Their Local Pastor," *Christianity Today*, January 5, 2018, https://tinyurl.com/ybbe5ask.

2 Throughout this book, I am referring to church not simply to indicate the institution of the church, or congregations, practices, and expressions of the church. Church is the body of Christ, not able to be pinned down by the practices, expressions, or community in any one form. It is global and eternal, not limited by our theologies, traditions, denominations, languages, or even life spans. Church outlasts nations, and church lives beyond the rise and fall of various institutional expressions of it. It is the people of God who find their identity in Christ and follow Jesus, bound together not by our efforts but by the Holy Spirit. Church is one body, with one God, one faith (Eph 4:4–6). We "church" in lots of ways, but church is bigger than all of them.

Chapter 2

1 There were years of emotional and structural cleanup, including paying some consultants thousands of dollars to produce a report detailing what went wrong. Six years later, when I was taking a seminary class called "Grief, Loss, Death and Dying," I decided to write a paper looking back at the experience and its impact on me. I contacted one of the consultants and requested to see the report. At first he agreed. Then he called back to say he had looked into the matter and I would not be permitted to view it.

2 I have shared my story and my experience of salvation in the midst of this experience. I am not speaking for Jenny, or her children or husband. Her loss was terrible and tragic. I can't say how God encountered her family during or after her death. I can only speak of my experience, and how God met me in my own place of need.

Chapter 3

1 My husband talks about this experience in his book, *The Promise of Despair*, and has used it often in public presentations. We may remember slight details differently.

2 Jason Wire, "20 Awesomely Untranslatable Words from around the World," Matador Network, October 5, 2010, https://tinyurl.com/y5wm6tk6.

3 I am indebted to logophile Carolyn Cochrane for this insight into the word *belong*.

4 See more on baptism in chapter 8.

Chapter 4

1 Andrew Root, *The Children of Divorce* (Grand Rapids, MI: Baker Academic, 2010).

Chapter 5

1 For these thoughts, I'm indebted to the late, great professor Ray Anderson, who lived in grace in his own life and, in his class lectures, delighted in exploring with us how grace works.

Chapter 6

1 Six months into the one-year experiment, we realized we could not go back; we had changed too much. Whatever else happened next would be a move forward rather than a return to what was. This was difficult for some of us who were game to try this for a year but were counting on the experiment ending and things returning to "normal." So we broke the whole congregation into listening groups, and with some nonviolent communication (NVC) training, the session/council listened to people's experiences for their feelings and needs. What needs were being met? What needs were not being met? Then the leadership shared what they had heard with the whole congregation. It turned out that many of the same needs (such as beauty, inspiration, and connection) were being met for some and unmet for others by the change. While there was grief over the loss of the rhythm of weekly Sunday morning worship, there was also vision and creativity and depth of spirituality developing in us through the new pattern. We were being changed and opened up through this new pattern of worship times. The congregation decided to continue in the new pattern while taking some intentional steps to remain mindful of our connection to each other and seeking to meet needs for belonging and beauty in other ways. This is an ongoing process of learning to hold each other's grief and joy, even and especially when the grief and joy result from the same shared experience.

2 In addition to Muller's book *Sabbath*, our thinking has been significantly shaped by Walter Brueggemann's *Sabbath as Resistance*. I also love to point people to two chapters on Sabbath, one from Barbara Brown Taylor's book *An Altar in the World* and the other from Ruth Haley Barton's *Sacred Rhythms*. I recommend an article by my friend (pastor, author, and chef) Simon Holt, "Slow Time in a Fast World: A Spirituality of Rest," *Ministry, Society and Theology* 16, no. 2 (2002): 10–21, https://tinyurl.com/y5nvnb74, which I share with folks all the time. You can see more about our congregation's practice of Sabbath and the theology behind it in an article I wrote for Luther Seminary's *Word & World* journal: Kara K. Root, "Sabbath: The Gift of Rest," *Word & World* 36, no. 3 (Summer 2016): https://tinyurl.com/y5vjh9cr.

3 "Time for a Digital Detox? Americans Check Their Phones 80 Times a *Day* While on Vacation—and More Than Half Have *Never* Unplugged When Taking Time Off," *Daily Mail*, May 17, 2018, https://tinyurl.com/yy3lwjvt; Meghan McCarty Carino, "American Workers Can Suffer Vacation Guilt . . . If They Take Vacations at All," *Marketplace*, July 12, 2019, https://tinyurl.com/y537beam.

Chapter 7

1 He talks about this in an interview with The Work of the People: Walter Brueggemann, "Scripts," interview by The Work of the People, accessed November 6, 2020, https://www.theworkofthepeople.com/scripts.

2 James C. Howell, *What Does the Lord Require? Doing Justice, Loving Kindness, Walking Humbly* (Louisville, KY: Westminster John Knox, 2012).

3 Mary Oliver, "The Summer Day," in *New and Selected Poems* (Boston: Beacon Press, 1992).

Chapter 8

1 As discussed in *The Pastor in a Secular Age* (2019) and *Faith Formation in a Secular Age* (2017) from Root's Ministry in a Secular Age series and *The End of Youth Ministry* (2020), all published by Baker Academic.

2 Rebecca Puhl, "Weight Discrimination Is Rampant. Yet in Most Places It's Still Legal," *Washington Post*, June 21, 2019, https://tinyurl.com/y22eku9r; Carey Goldberg, "Study: Bias Drops Dramatically for Sexual Orientation and Race—but Not Weight," WBUR, January 11, 2019, https://tinyurl.com/y8evh7os.

3 See Dennis Sanders, *The Clockwork Pastor* (blog), https://questorpastor.wordpress.com/.

4 In this moment, heaven and earth converge in the person of Christ. Jesus is God, fully God. That is his identity. And the full God shuffles into the waters of humanity, submitting anonymously, alongside everyone else, to this act of repentance and renewal—for that is what John's baptism was. God claims his identity as a human being, a distinctly *not God* creature in need of God. And at the same time that the human Jesus reaches out toward the Divine, the divinity of God reaches out and claims Jesus with a voice from heaven and blessing, and the Holy Spirit wraps the connection in affirmation, pronouncement, and blessing. The Trinity is on full display in the movement of God toward us and us toward God. Every Christian tradition acts out that movement, by the way. Whether by dedicating babies and baptizing adults, or baptizing babies and confirming a person later, all traditions express the covenant movement of God claiming us and our responding yes to God's Yes.

5 This is another story that Andy uses regularly, and again, we may remember details slightly differently.

6 Rowan Williams speaks to this beautifully throughout his book *Being Disciples* (Grand Rapids, MI: Eerdmans, 2016).

Chapter 9

1 See Patheos (website), accessed November 6, 2020, https://www .patheos.com. For "Why I Need the Resurrection," see Patheos Editors, "Why I Need the Resurrection," Patheos, March 31, 2010, https://tinyurl.com/y2jwpkgm. For "Is the Resurrection for Real?" see Patheos Contributors, "Is the Resurrection for Real?," Patheos, April 18, 2011, https://tinyurl.com/yxk6su3h.

2 Patheos Contributors, "Is the Resurrection for Real?"

3 Richard Carlson, "Commentary on 1 Corinthians 15:19–26," Preach This Week, Working Preacher, March 27, 2016, https:// tinyurl.com/yyo55k7a.

4 My original response was published on Patheos in 2010 (see Patheos Editors, "Why I Need the Resurrection"); this version was adapted for a sermon preached to the Lake Nokomis Presbyterian Church (LNPC) congregation August 21, 2016.

Chapter 10

1 I'm indebted to my friend Phil GebbenGreen for this wording.

2 Shared in James Finley, *Merton's Palace of Nowhere*, 40th anniversary edition (1978; Notre Dame, IN: Ave Maria Press, 2018).

Chapter 11

1 In this book I have told my story. This comes from my perspective and is drawn from my experiences. I have no doubt that were my sisters and my parents each to tell their stories, they would be quite different from mine. Their stories come from their perspectives and are drawn from their experiences—some of which were shared between us, and some of which were theirs alone. "There is a reason there are four gospel accounts in the Bible!" my friend Jodi Houge says,

and our understanding of who God is and what God is up to is all the richer for it. I recognize that life is a story—made up of our experiences and our interpretation of those experiences, which is to say, life is the stories we tell ourselves about our life as much as it is the collection of moments we actually live. We can't often change our experiences, but we can change our stories. I believe that begins with approaching our lives with deep compassion, vulnerable courage, and genuine curiosity. I have sincerely tried to do this in sharing my story. I hope that in doing so, I have also honored my family and left room for readers to imagine their stories as different from mine.

2 This is explored in depth in Haley Goranson Jacobs, *Conformed to the Image of His Son: Reconsidering Paul's Theology of Glory in Romans* (Downers Grove, IL: IVP Academic, 2018).